The Cambridge Introduction to
Nathaniel Hawthorne

As the author of *The Scarlet Letter*, Nathaniel Hawthorne has been established as a major writer of the nineteenth century and the most prominent chronicler of New England and its colonial history. This introductory book for students coming to Hawthorne for the first time outlines his life and writings in a clear and accessible style. Leland S. Person also explains some of the significant cultural and social movements that influenced Hawthorne's most important writings: Puritanism, Transcendentalism, and Feminism. The major works, including *The Scarlet Letter*, *The House of the Seven Gables*, and *The Blithedale Romance*, as well as Hawthorne's important short stories and non-fiction, are analyzed in detail. The book also includes a brief history and survey of Hawthorne scholarship, with special emphasis on recent studies. Students of nineteenth-century American literature will find this a rewarding and engaging introduction to this remarkable writer.

Leland S. Person is Professor of English at the University of Cincinnati.

Cambridge Introductions to Literature

This series is designed to introduce students to key topics and authors. Accessible and lively, these introductions will also appeal to readers who want to broaden their understanding of the books and authors they enjoy.

- Ideal for students, teachers, and lecturers
- Concise, yet packed with essential information
- Key suggestions for further reading

The Cambridge Introduction to
Nathaniel Hawthorne

LELAND S. PERSON

CAMBRIDGE
UNIVERSITY PRESS

CAMBRIDGE UNIVERSITY PRESS

Cambridge, New York, Melbourne, Madrid, Cape Town, Singapore, São Paulo

Cambridge University Press
The Edinburgh Building, Cambridge CB2 8RU, UK

Published in the United States of America by Cambridge University Press, New York

www.cambridge.org
Information on this title: www.cambridge.org/9780521670968

First published 2007

Printed in the United Kingdom at the University Press, Cambridge

A catalogue record for this publication is available from the British Library

Library of Congress Cataloguing in Publication data
Person, Leland S.
The Cambridge introduction to Nathaniel Hawthorne / Leland S. Person.
    p.   cm.
Includes bibliographical references and index.
ISBN-13: 978-0-521-85458-0 (alk. paper)
ISBN-10: 0-521-85458-X (alk. paper)
ISBN-13: 978-0-521-67096-8 (pbk. : alk. paper)
ISBN-10: 0-521-67096-9 (pbk. : alk. paper)
1. Hawthorne, Nathaniel, 1804–1864 – Criticism and interpretation.   I. Title.
PS1888.P47   2007
813′.3 dc22   2006036015

ISBN 978-0-521-85458-0 (hardback)
ISBN 978-0-521-67096-8 (paperback)

Contents

Chapter 4 Hawthorne's novels 66

Chapter 5 Hawthorne's critics 114

A note on the texts

In quoting from Hawthorne's writing, I have used *The Centenary Edition of the Works of Nathaniel Hawthorne*, ed. William Charvat et al., 23 vols. (Columbus: Ohio State University Press, 1962–97). I have cited quotations from this edition by volume and page number.

Vol. 1: *The Scarlet Letter* (1962)
Vol. 2: *The House of the Seven Gables* (1965)
Vol. 3: *The Blithedale Romance and Fanshawe* (1964)
Vol. 4: *The Marble Faun: or, The Romance of Monte Beni* (1968)
Vol. 5: *Our Old Home: A Series of English Sketches* (1970)
Vol. 6: *True Stories from History and Biography* (1972)
Vol. 7: *A Wonder Book and Tanglewood Tales* (1972)
Vol. 8: *The American Notebooks* (1972)
Vol. 9: *Twice-Told Tales* (1974)
Vol. 10: *Mosses from an Old Manse* (1974)
Vol. 11: *The Snow Image and Uncollected Tales* (1974)
Vol. 12: *The American Claimant Manuscripts* (1977)
Vol. 13: *The Elixir of Life Manuscripts* (1977)
Vol. 14: *The French and Italian Notebooks* (1980)
Vol. 15: *The Letters, 1813–1843* (1984)
Vol. 16: *The Letters, 1843–1853* (1985)
Vol. 17: *The Letters, 1853–1856* (1987)
Vol. 18: *The Letters, 1857–1864* (1987)
Vol. 19: *The Consular Letters, 1853–1855* (1988)
Vol. 20: *The Consular Letters, 1856–1857* (1988)
Vol. 21: *The English Notebooks, 1853–1856* (1997)
Vol. 22: *The English Notebooks, 1856–1860* (1997)
Vol. 23: *Miscellaneous Prose and Verse* (1995)

Preface

Even people who have not read Hawthorne's *The Scarlet Letter* know about scarlet letters. In building a novel around the predicament of a Puritan woman, Hester Prynne, who is punished for her crime of adultery by being made to wear a scarlet A on her dress, Hawthorne gave us a convenient way of thinking about crime and punishment and about our power to make sentences fit the nature of crimes. We see many references to scarlet letters in the popular media.

Hawthorne is also popularly associated with Puritanism, and he did set some of his best-known fictions, including *The Scarlet Letter,* in the seventeenth-century world of Puritan New England. One of his ancestors had been a judge at the Salem witchcraft trials in 1692, and Hawthorne said he felt guilty about his ancestor's role in persecuting some of Salem's citizens. Hawthorne did not confine himself to Puritanism, however. He was a master psychologist, and many of his works focus on individuals' efforts to understand complex moral problems and relationships.

Hawthorne had an unusual career in that he wrote nothing but short fiction for twenty years and then, after publishing *The Scarlet Letter* in 1850, nothing but novels for the last fifteen years of his career. *The Scarlet Letter* was a modest bestseller, and he tried to capitalize on its success by writing *The House of the Seven Gables, The Blithedale Romance,* and *The Marble Faun.* Many of his early stories still have the power to puzzle and fascinate us – especially "My Kinsman, Major Molineux," "Roger Malvin's Burial," "Young Goodman Brown," "The Minister's Black Veil," "Wakefield," "The Birth-mark," and "Rappaccini's Daughter" – and I have devoted chapter 3 to those and other short works. In chapter 4, I analyze each of the four major novels from several different angles, reflecting a few of the approaches Hawthorne's critics have employed. In chapter 1 I highlight the most important events in Hawthorne's life, with special emphasis on places where his life and his fiction seem to intersect. Since critical approaches to Hawthorne's work increasingly emphasize the historical, social, and political context in which he wrote, I have placed his writing in five relevant contexts in chapter 2 (Puritanism, Transcendentalism, Feminism, Race and Slavery, and Nineteenth-century Manhood). Chapter 5 provides brief summaries of key critical works, with special emphasis on recent criticism, and also includes suggestions for further, in-depth reading.

I have spent thirty years reading, teaching, and writing about Hawthorne. In this introduction I have tried as much as possible to write about Hawthorne the way I teach him – always aware that there are many different ways. Just as the scarlet letter comes to mean different things to different people, *The Scarlet Letter* and Hawthorne's other fiction can be read from many different angles.

Chapter 1

Hawthorne's life

Born on the Fourth of July in 1804, Nathaniel Hawthorne ranks with Herman
Melville, Henry James, and Mark Twain among the best nineteenth-century
American male novelists. Hawthorne grew up in Salem, Massachusetts, and
Puritan history provided him with the background for many of his later fictional
works, such as "The Gentle Boy" (1832), "Alice Doane's Appeal" (1835), "Young
Goodman Brown" (1835), "The May-Pole of Merry Mount" (1836), "The Man
of Adamant" (1837), "Endicott and the Red Cross" (1838), and of course *The
Scarlet Letter* (actually set in Boston during the 1640s). In this novel of a Puritan
community's marking and punishing of Hester Prynne, Hawthorne provided
us with a reference point for understanding many twentieth-century examples
of scapegoating and social ostracism.

Hawthorne's sea-captain father died at sea when he was only four, and he
was raised by his mother and her family, the Mannings. When his mother
moved to Raymond, Maine, in 1819, he stayed in Salem with his uncle's family
and did not see her for two years. He entered Bowdoin College in Brunswick,
Maine, in the fall of 1821 at the age of seventeen. He was not a stellar student.
Shortly after his matriculation, he wrote his uncle William that the "Laws of
the College are not at all too strict, and I do not have to study near so hard
as I did in Salem" (15: 155). Hawthorne did find some rules "repugnant" –
especially those involving religion. He resented having to "get up at sunrise
every morning to attend prayers," although he noted that the students "make
it a custom" to break that law "twice a week." "But worst of all," he told his
sister Louisa, "is to be compelled to go to meeting every Sunday, and to hear a
red hot Calvinist Sermon from the President, or some other dealer in fire and
brimstone" (15: 159). Hawthorne found other rules less strict, but they did
catch up with him. In May 1822, he had to write his mother that he had been
caught playing cards and had been fined fifty cents (15: 171). Since some of
the card players were suspended, Hawthorne appears to have gotten off lightly,
the college president apparently believing, Hawthorne later noted, that he had
been led "away by the wicked ones." In this, Hawthorne boasted to Louisa,
"he is greatly mistaken. I was full as willing to play as the person he suspects

of having enticed me, and would have been influenced by no one. I have a great mind to commence playing again, merely to show him that I scorn to be seduced by another into anything wrong" (15: 174). Hawthorne graduated from Bowdoin in the summer of 1824. Like a lot of students then and now, he had formed no particular plans for his post-graduate life. In his last letter from Bowdoin he reflected philosophically on his college experience and his prospects:

> The family had before conceived much too high an opinion of my talents, and had probably formed expectations, which I shall never realise [sic]. I have thought much upon the subject, and have finally come to the conclusion, that I shall never make a distinguished figure in the world, and all I hope or wish to do is to plod along with the multitude.   (15: 194)

Hawthorne undoubtedly underplays what he had learned at Bowdoin. His first novel *Fanshawe* derived from his college experience and confirmed him in the profession of authorship he had tentatively marked out for himself before he matriculated. "I have not yet concluded what profession I shall have," he wrote his mother in March 1821. Being a minister sounded too "dull." There are so many lawyers that half of them "are in a state of actual starvation." Being a physician would mean living "by the diseases and Infirmities" of his "fellow Creatures" (15: 139). He wonders, therefore,

> What would you think of my becoming an Author, and relying for support upon my pen. Indeed I think the illegibility of my handwriting is very authorlike. How proud you would feel to see my works praised by the reviewers, as equal to proudest productions of the scribbling sons of John Bull.   (15: 139)

Hawthorne wrote prophetically, although he could not have known it at the time; for it took him many years – sixteen – to put his name on a book he had written (*Twice-Told Tales* in 1837). In many respects, Hawthorne took nothing more important away from Bowdoin than the friendships he made there. His classmate Franklin Pierce became a lifelong friend and went on to become President of the United States. Hawthorne would write Pierce's campaign biography, and Pierce would reward him by appointing him American Consul in Liverpool, the most lucrative job Hawthorne would ever have. Another classmate, Horatio Bridge, would secretly subsidize the publication of *Twice-Told Tales* and would agree to let Hawthorne edit the journal he kept as a US Naval officer and member of the first expedition to intercept slave-traders off the coast of Africa. *The Journal of an African Cruiser* would appear in 1845 with Hawthorne's name alone on the cover. A third classmate, poet Henry Wadsworth Longfellow, would write a very favorable review of *Twice-Told Tales* and also become a lifelong friend and supporter.

Hawthorne enjoyed considerable success after the publication of *The Scarlet Letter* in 1850, but he struggled during the first decade of his career to achieve even modest success. He attempted to promote three different collections of linked tales (*Seven Tales of My Native Land*, *Provincial Tales*, and *The Story Teller*), but he settled for anonymous publication of individual stories and sketches in such periodicals as *The New England Magazine* and in annual gift books, such as Samuel Goodrich's *The Token*. If not quite the "obscurest man of letters in America," as he would later style himself, he enjoyed little public reputation before 1837 (9: 3).

With the publication of *Twice-Told Tales*, however, Hawthorne emerged as an important writer whose national reputation grew steadily through the following decades. In every respect, the late 1830s represent the watershed moment in Hawthorne's personal and professional life – the period of his first real professional success and of his engagement to Sophia Peabody (the first surviving love letter dates from 6 March 1839).

He got his first real job in 1839 when he became a measurer at the Boston Custom House, earning $1,500 a year, and he began a pattern that would continue for most of his lifetime: when he worked outside the home he wrote relatively little; when he had no job he wrote prolifically. Brenda Wineapple believes that "Hawthorne held on to his government job not just because he needed the money or because the country ignored its artists – though both were true – but because he liked it."[1] He especially liked the male camaraderie. The working experience was not uniformly positive, however, and Hawthorne complained to Sophia of the dehumanizing effects of his job. "I am a machine," he observed, "and am surrounded by hundreds of similar machines; – or rather, all of the business people are so many wheels of one great machine" (15: 330).

Hawthorne met Sophia Peabody in 1838, beginning a three-and-half-year courtship that ended in marriage on 9 July 1842. The 109 surviving love letters that Hawthorne wrote to Sophia before their wedding reveal not only his intense feelings but also the high hopes he had for his ability to be both a husband and a writer. Although allowances should be made for a lover's enthusiasm, the letters testify to Sophia's remarkable power to make him know himself. In a well-known letter from 4 October 1840, for example, he admits, "I used to think that I could imagine all passions, all feelings, all states of the heart and mind; but how little did I know what it is to be mingled with another's being! Thou only hast taught me that I have a heart – thou only hast thrown a light deep downward, and upward, into my soul" (15: 495). Hawthorne anticipates the language he uses at the beginning of *The Scarlet Letter*. There, as he reflected upon his relationship to the novel he had written, he conceived of it as a type of love letter, an agent for his male ego that would court that "one heart and mind of perfect sympathy" from which he felt himself divided. The "printed book," he could imagine, might "find out the divided segment of the writer's own nature, and complete his circle of existence by bringing him into communion with it" (1: 3–4). Writing and relationship – both were creative. As he told Sophia in the same letter of 4 October:

> Thou only hast revealed me to myself; for without thy aid, my best knowledge of myself would have been merely to know my own shadow – to watch it flickering on the wall, and mistake its fantasies for my own real actions. Indeed, we are but shadows – we are not endowed with real life, and all that seems most real about us is but the thinnest substance of a dream – till the heart is touched. That touch creates us – then we begin to be – thereby we are beings of reality, and inheritors of eternity.   (15: 495)

Hawthorne was thirty-six when he wrote this letter. His zeal suggests a long-standing ideal belatedly realized, a change within himself that must have seemed like a rebirth. Courtship and marriage, he believed, would kindle his imagination and cause an outpouring of literary production. In the hope of combining work and creativity and discovering a home for himself and Sophia, Hawthorne resigned his job at the Boston Custom House in January 1841 and soon took up residence at Brook Farm, a utopian community founded by George Ripley in West Roxbury, Massachusetts. In the interim, he wrote two books for children, *Famous Old People* and *Liberty Tree*, which, along with *Grandfather's Chair*, were published by his soon-to-be sister-in-law, Elizabeth Peabody (Wineapple, 143). Initially Hawthorne's spirits soared at Brook Farm, despite the hard physical labor. This morning "I have done wonders," he would exclaim to Sophia on April 14. "Before breakfast, I went out to the barn, and began to chop hay for the cattle. . . Then I brought wood and replenished the fires; and finally sat down to breakfast and ate up a huge mound of buckwheat cakes." Hawthorne could even celebrate the less pleasant aspects of the work. "After breakfast," he continued, "Mr. Ripley put a four-pronged instrument into my hands, which he gave me to understand was called a pitch-fork; and he and Mr. Farley being armed with similar weapons, we all three commenced a gallant attack upon a heap of manure" (15: 528). References to shoveling manure, which Hawthorne called the "gold mine," became a running joke in the letters he wrote from the Farm. Hawthorne struggled to situate himself in positive terms within a limited matrix of acceptable nineteenth-century male identities, so it is not surprising that the Brook Farm letters emphasize the benefits of physical labor on his body. The experience gave him the simple pleasure of identifying himself as a manual laborer. "I shall make an excellent husbandman," he punned to Sophia. "I feel the original Adam reviving within me" (15: 529). In fact, he allowed his writing ability to be eclipsed by his growing physical prowess, proudly complaining to Sophia on 22 April that he was scribbling in "an abominable hand" because he had been chopping wood and turning a grindstone all morning, and the exertion had been likely to "disturb the equilibrium of the muscles and sinews" (15: 533). Two weeks later he would brag, "I have gained strength wonderfully – grown quite a giant, in fact – and can do a day's work without the slightest inconvenience" (15: 539).

Brief though it was, Hawthorne's experience at Brook Farm not only provided him with raw material (in the form of notebook passages) for *The Blithedale Romance*, published a decade later, but it gave him the chance to test his belief in various ideas about work and community. Among other things, Brook Farmers wanted to liberate labor and laborers from conditions they regarded as virtual enslavement in order to "insure," in Ripley's words, a "more natural union between intellectual and manual labor than now exists; to combine the thinker and the worker, as far as possible, in the same individual; to guarantee the highest mental freedom, by providing all with labor, adapted to their tastes and talents, and securing to them the fruits of their industry."[2] Hawthorne wanted to believe in this agenda, and he did his best to spiritualize even the most onerous labor. "I have been at work under the clear blue sky, on a hill side," he wrote Sophia on 4 May. "Sometimes it almost seemed as if I were at work in the sky itself; though the material in which I wrought was the ore from our gold mine." Using his imagination and his pen alchemically, Hawthorne turns "lead" into gold. Anticipating Walt Whitman's ecological organicism in "Song of Myself" and other poems, Hawthorne assures Sophia, "there is nothing so unseemly and disagreeable in this sort of toil, as thou wouldst think. It defiles the hands, indeed, but not the soul. This gold ore is a pure and wholesome substance; else our Mother Nature would not devour it so readily, and derive so much nourishment from it, and return such a rich abundance of good grain and roots in requital of it" (15: 542).

Brook Farm failed in part because the community never attracted enough farmers to allow the release from labor that the founders intended. Hawthorne came to the conclusion that he would spend most of his time and energy in physical labor and thus be unable to write. As early as 1 June, his view of the farm changed drastically. "I think this present life of mine gives me an antipathy to pen and ink, even more than my Custom House experience did," he admitted, and he went on to call it the "worst" of "all hateful places," fearing that his soul might be "buried and perish under a dung-heap or in a furrow of the field" (15: 545). He liked outdoor work and liked the idea of a balance between work and writing, but the farm took virtually all of his time and mental energy. "My former stories all sprung up of their own accord, out of a quiet life," he told his friend George Hillard. "Now, I have no quiet at all; for when my outward man is at rest – which is seldom, and for short intervals – my mind is bothered with a sort of dull excitement, which makes it impossible to think continuously of any subject" (15: 550). He was coming to see his situation as a form of "bondage" (15: 557). He worried about becoming "brutified" (15: 558) and transformed into a "slave" (15: 559), and he soon left Brook Farm for good.

Without employment, Hawthorne embarked upon several publishing projects, including the second edition of *Twice-Told Tales* and *Biographical Stories for Children*, while he planned for his marriage to Sophia. He arranged with Emerson to rent his family's Old Manse in Concord, and he and Sophia moved in on their wedding day (9 July 1842). Situated on the banks of the Concord River and overlooking the site of the Old North Bridge and the first battleground of the Revolutionary War, the Old Manse stimulated Hawthorne's imagination. The three years he spent in Concord (July 1842–November 1845) represent a fascinating period in his life. Concord in the 1840s was a kind of intellectual utopian community and included a remarkable gathering of intellectual and artistic personalities: Emerson, Thoreau, Margaret Fuller, Bronson Alcott, Ellery Channing, and others whom we now associate with the Transcendentalist, abolitionist, women's suffrage, and other reform movements. These friendships have provided Hawthorne's modern readers with much food for speculation about influence, rivalry, and cross-pollination.[3] Hawthorne's notebooks record numerous visits and outings that, if time travel were a possibility, literary scholars would pay dearly to observe.

During the first winter at the Manse, for example, the meadow at the foot of their orchard froze over, and one of Sophia's letters describes Hawthorne skating with Emerson and Thoreau. "Do you know how majestically he skates?" she would tell Louisa Hawthorne. "He looks very kingly, wrapt in his cloak, gliding to & fro" (15: 667). Hawthorne loved the opportunity for such recreation. He would tell Margaret Fuller, "I have skated like a very schoolboy, this winter. Indeed, since my marriage, the circle of my life seems to have come round, and brought back many of my school-day enjoyments; and I find a deeper pleasure in them now than when I first went over them. I pause upon them, and taste them with a sort of epicurism, and am boy and man together" (15: 671).

Hawthorne especially liked Thoreau. Describing Thoreau as a "wild, irregular, Indian-like sort of fellow," Hawthorne praised his writing as the product of a "genuine and exquisite observer of nature – a character almost as rare as that of a true poet" (15: 656). Thoreau "seems inclined to lead a sort of Indian life among civilized men," Hawthorne wrote in his notebook, "an Indian life, I mean, as respects the absence of any systematic effort for a livelihood" (8: 354). Hawthorne bought the boat that Thoreau and his brother John had used for their trip on the Concord and Merrimack Rivers in 1839, changing the name from *Musketaquid* to *Pond Lily*, and he has fun at his own expense in contrasting Thoreau's rowing ability with his own. Whereas Thoreau "managed the boat so perfectly, either with two paddles or with one, that it seemed instinct with his own will" (8: 355–56), Hawthorne notes that "the boat seemed to be bewitched" when he tried to row it, and "turned its head to every point of the compass except the right one" (8: 356). When Thoreau decided to visit Staten Island in the spring of 1843, Hawthorne wished that Thoreau would remain in Concord, "he being one of the few persons, I think, with whom to hold intercourse is like hearing the wind among the boughs of a forest-tree" (8: 369). Hawthorne visited Thoreau at his Walden Pond cabin and, after moving to Salem, arranged for him to lecture at the Salem Lyceum on two occasions. Thoreau read an early version of "Economy," the first chapter of what would become *Walden* (1854).

In *Hawthorne's Fuller Mystery*, Thomas Mitchell has carefully analyzed Hawthorne's relationship with Margaret Fuller, and he details the times they spent together during the Concord years.[4] Mitchell argues for Fuller's profound influence on Hawthorne and his writing, especially on such characters as Beatrice Rappaccini, Hester Prynne, Zenobia in *The Blithedale Romance*, and Miriam Schaefer in *The Marble Faun*. Hawthorne's letters and notebooks record many visits that Fuller paid to the Old Manse, and he described one remarkable meeting with Fuller in a lengthy notebook entry for 22 August 1842. Fuller was staying with the Emersons, and Hawthorne set out after dinner to return a book she had left at the Manse. Fuller was not home when he called, but he encountered her on his return journey through the woods in Sleepy Hollow. Sitting by Margaret's side, Hawthorne would note, "we talked about Autumn – and about the pleasures of getting lost in the woods – and about the crows, whose voices Margaret had heard . . . and about the sight of mountains from a distance, and the view from their summits – and about other matters of high and low philosophy" (8: 343). As Mitchell has argued, this scene and passage may provide a basis for the forest scene in *The Scarlet Letter* in which Hester Prynne and Arthur Dimmesdale make their plans to leave Boston. Hester famously declares, "What we did had a consecration of its own. We felt it so! We said so to each other!" (1: 195). Hawthorne and Fuller were interrupted by none other than Emerson, "who, in spite of his clerical consecration, had found no better way of spending the Sabbath than to ramble among the woods" (8: 343). The word "consecration" links the two passages and can fuel speculations about what was going through Hawthorne's mind when he wrote the scene in the novel.

Hawthorne never warmed to Emerson, and the conventional wisdom is that he disliked Concord's most famous citizen, perhaps resenting the attention Emerson received as philosopher-in-residence. But Hawthorne made several excursions with Emerson that bespeak a good friendship – a walk one Sunday in August 1842 to Walden Pond, a two-day walking trip later that fall to Harvard, Massachusetts, and then to a Shaker village three miles beyond (8: 361–62). On 3 April 1843, when Sophia was visiting her family in Salem, Hawthorne entertained Emerson at the Manse. Emerson appeared "with a sunbeam in his face," Hawthorne wrote, "and we had as good a talk as I ever remember experiencing with him." Emerson especially wanted to talk about Fuller, whom he "apotheosized" as the "greatest woman" of ancient or modern times, but the two men also discussed Thoreau and Brook Farm (8: 371).

One of the most remarkable events that occurred while the Hawthornes lived in Concord – especially important for its incorporation into *The Blithedale Romance* – involved the suicidal drowning of nineteen-year-old Martha Hunt in the Concord River, not far from the Old Manse. The incident occurred on July 9, 1845 – the Hawthornes' third wedding anniversary – and it takes some feat of imagination to see Hawthorne, on the night of his anniversary, out in a boat, dragging the river for Martha Hunt's body and devoting nine handwritten pages to the experience in his notebook. He would transfer the lengthy account almost verbatim into *The Blithedale Romance*, substituting Zenobia for Martha Hunt, but otherwise hardly changing his original account – probing for the body with a long pole, hauling it to the surface, trying in vain to force her rigid arms down to her sides (8: 263). Hawthorne wrote compulsively about the incident, which in the context of his wedding anniversary surely provided a traumatic example of love and death conjoined that he would build into the novel he wrote seven years later.

Although Hawthorne wrote very little during his courtship of Sophia (he was working hard to make marriage economically feasible), the Old Manse period resulted in the publication of twenty-one new tales and sketches, including "The Birth-mark," "Egotism; or, the Bosom Serpent," "The Celestial Railroad," "The Artist of the Beautiful," "Drowne's Wooden Image," and "Rappaccini's Daughter." Marriage gave him an economic motive to publish, and a settled domestic life gave him the opportunity, but most important, his relationship with Sophia inspired him to center his attention, more than he ever had before, on the creative possibilities and the problems of relationship.

Despite the wedded bliss expressed in "The New Adam and Eve" (one of the first stories he wrote at the Manse) and in some of Hawthorne's letters and notebook entries, however, "The Birth-mark," "The Artist of the Beautiful," and "Rappaccini's Daughter" depict vexed and dangerous male–female relationships in which male characters direct violent impulses toward women. Georgiana in "The Birth-mark" and Beatrice in "Rappaccini's Daughter" both die, at least in part because of male actions. It is always risky to read fiction biographically, but it is tempting in these cases to speculate that something in Hawthorne's situation was provoking serious anxiety and causing him to struggle imaginatively with the tensions he felt between being a writer and being a husband and father.

Several letters he wrote after Una's birth (3 March 1844) express bewilderment at his paternity. In a letter to his sister Louisa he admitted that he was "almost afraid to look" at the baby (16: 15), and even six weeks later he still doubted his fatherhood. Una, he said, "has not yet sufficiently realized herself in my soul; it seems like a dream, therefore, which needs such assurances as thy letter, to convince me that it is more than a dream" (16: 29). Fatherhood did force Hawthorne to think more pragmatically about his career, intensifying the pressure he felt to write simply in order to provide for his family and making him more concerned with writing as a business.

Hawthorne left the Old Manse and Concord because he could not afford to live there. Magazine publication paid poorly, and the Hawthornes struggled to pay rent on the Old Manse, especially after Una's birth. Friends such as Franklin Pierce, Horatio Bridge, and John O'Sullivan tried to help by finding Hawthorne another government job. The only option Hawthorne could imagine was to return home – to Salem and the Manning house. Five months later, he finally secured a lucrative political appointment from President James K. Polk as Surveyor of the Salem Custom House. His yearly earnings approached $1,200. He must have breathed a huge sigh of relief.

By the time Julian was born (22 June 1846), therefore, Hawthorne felt much better about himself as both a man and a father. He did not have to worry about making his writing support the family, and he wrote little during the Custom House period (1846–49). Hawthorne kept his position as Surveyor for three years, until the election of the Whig Zachary Taylor to the Presidency resulted in his firing in the summer of 1849. Hawthorne and his friends tried unsuccessfully to retain the Surveyor's position amid increasingly politicized accusations of corruption. Hawthorne protested that he had not been "appointed to office as a reward for political services," nor had he "acted as a politician since" (16: 263), and he vowed to "immolate" his critics if they should succeed in getting him out of office (16: 269). "I may perhaps select a victim," he wrote to Longfellow, "and let fall one little drop of venom on his heart, that shall make him writhe before the grin of the multitude for a considerable time to come" (16: 270).

Hawthorne announced on June 8, 1849, that he had been "turned out of office" (16: 273), and he writes Longfellow that it feels as if his "head has been chopt off" (16:283). He would use the same image in "The Custom-House" when he termed the collection of which *The Scarlet Letter* was originally intended to form a part, the "POSTHUMOUS PAPERS OF A DECAPITATED SURVEYOR" (1: 43). Adding to Hawthorne's dark mood was the death of his mother on 31 July.

He would have his revenge on his political enemies in *The Scarlet Letter*, the novel he sat down to write almost immediately after he lost his job as Surveyor. He would tell his publisher, James T. Fields, that in the process of writing, "all political and official turmoil has subsided within me, so that I have not felt inclined to execute justice on any of my enemies" (16: 305), but most scholars think Hawthorne merely sublimated his anger in his depiction of the Puritans who, though actually members of the Massachusetts Bay colony, stand in for the Salemites with whom Hawthorne felt angry. Many readers have seen a connection between Hawthorne and his heroine, whose punishment and ostracism from the Puritan community force her to eke out a living as a kind of artist.

Hawthorne worked on *The Scarlet Letter* during the fall and winter of 1849–50, and its publication in the spring (16 March) inaugurated the most productive period in his writing career, as he published eight books in the first four years of the 1850s. Moving to Lenox in western Massachusetts in the autumn of that year, Hawthorne wrote and published *The House of the Seven Gables*. Trading on his increasing popularity, he collected his earlier children's fiction as *True Stories from History and Biography*, wrote a new volume of children's stories, *A Wonder Book for Girls and Boys*, and also published a final collection of short fiction, *The Snow-Image, and Other Twice-Told Tales*. On 5 August 1850, he joined a party to climb Monument Mountain in Stockbridge, Massachusetts, where he met Herman Melville, who would soon buy an old farmhouse in Pittsfield and rapidly develop into a close friend. "Before the day was over," Melville biographer Hershel Parker notes, "Melville decided Hawthorne was the most fascinating American he had ever met," and for his part, Hawthorne "did something phenomenal. He liked Melville so much that he asked him to spend a few days with him."[5]

Many scholars believe that the rapidly developing friendship with Hawthorne, as well as the positive reinforcement Hawthorne's example provided to write from the heart, significantly influenced *Moby-Dick* (1851), the novel on which Melville was working. Melville dedicated *Moby-Dick* to

"Nathaniel Hawthorne. In Token of My Admiration for His Genius," and several of his letters to Hawthorne during this period testify to the older Hawthorne's influence.

Hawthorne's friendship with Melville has long fascinated critics and fueled considerable speculation. Although Hawthorne's letters to Melville during this period do not survive, more than a dozen of Melville's letters support scholarly attempts to characterize Melville's feelings – especially the letter Melville wrote after receiving Hawthorne's praise of *Moby-Dick*, with its "pantheistic" feeling of "divine magnanimities": "your heart beat in my ribs and mine in yours, and both in God's. A sense of unspeakable security is in me this moment, on account of your having understood the book."[6] Most famously, Edwin H. Miller argued that an "advance" from Melville that Hawthorne experienced as an "assault" caused the two writers to become estranged in 1851.[7] Few other scholars feel so confident about the biographical facts, even though nearly all acknowledge the passionate feelings Melville expressed. Parker calls Melville's review of *Mosses* a "passionate private message to his new friend," and he speculates that "writing so intimately about Hawthorne's power to arouse his literary aspirations had left him more than a little febrile – excited intellectually, emotionally, and sexually – sexual arousal being for Melville an integral part of such intensely creative phases."[8] Robert Milder dismisses for lack of evidence Miller's suggestion that Melville made a homoerotic "advance," and he concludes that Melville's attraction to Hawthorne "does not seem the object-cathexis of a free-floating homosexual disposition but a reaction to an extraordinary individual."[9] Critics have often examined *Pierre; or, The Ambiguities* and Hawthorne's *The Blithedale Romance* for clues about what transpired between the two men in the Berkshires, because they published these books in the immediate aftermath of their experience. Monica Mueller has devoted an entire book to the subject.[10] And in his provocative reading of *Pierre* as a "closeted" gay text, James Creech considers Hawthorne the "erotic model" for Isabel Banford, Pierre's half-sister (119).[11]

In view of Melville's praise for the "blackness" of Hawthorne's vision, Hawthorne's efforts to make *The House of the Seven Gables* a brighter book than *The Scarlet Letter* seem ironic, although he would comment as he neared completion that the book "darkens damnably towards the close," and he would have to "try hard to pour some setting sunshine over it" (16: 376). On the day he sent it off to his editor, James T. Fields, he said that he preferred it to *The Scarlet Letter* – in part because it had "met with extraordinary success from that portion of the public to whose judgment it has been submitted" – namely, Sophia (16: 386). Responding to Evert Duyckinck's positive review of the novel, Hawthorne claimed that it was a "more natural and healthy product" of his mind than *The Scarlet Letter* (16: 421). The novel solidified the reputation he had earned from *The Scarlet Letter* – and even sold a little better. Published by Ticknor, Reed, and Fields on 9 April 1851, *The House of the Seven Gables* sold 6,710 copies in its first year.[12]

Hawthorne could not have known it at the time, but when Rose was born in 1851 (May 20), events were already in motion that would change him drastically as a writer. The Hawthornes left Lenox in November 1851 for several reasons. He was tired of the little red house, which he once called "the most inconvenient and wretched little hovel" he had ever put his head in (16: 454). He missed the seacoast, thinking that it suited his "constitution" and Sophia's better than the "hill-country" (16: 462). He had also gotten into a spat with his landlady, Caroline Sturgis Tappan, over his right to the fruit on the property he was renting (16: 481–84).

After leaving western Massachusetts, the Hawthornes lived briefly in West Newton, where they rented a house from Sophia's sister Mary and brother-in-law, Horace Mann. Hawthorne's final collection of tales, *The Snow-Image, and Other Twice-Told Tales* was published (late in 1851), although the volume contained very few recent tales. Hawthorne also wrote *The Blithedale Romance* in West Newton, during the winter and spring of 1851–52. By the time the novel was published in July, Hawthorne was living back in Concord, although on the other side of town from the Old Manse, in a house he bought from Bronson Alcott (father of Louisa May Alcott) and "re-baptized" "The Wayside" for its "moral as well as descriptive propriety" (16: 548). Emerson lived just down the road.

When the Democratic Party nominated Franklin Pierce for President in June of 1852, Hawthorne wrote Pierce's campaign biography. Many members of Hawthorne's extended family, as well as many of his Concord neighbors, had little use for the moderate Pierce, especially because he refused to support abolitionism, and Hawthorne's alignment with Pierce was widely criticized. Scholars such as Jonathan Arac and Sacvan Bercovitch have used Hawthorne's characterization of Pierce's gradualist approach to slavery to argue that in his fiction (especially in *The Scarlet Letter*) Hawthorne himself expresses a conservative view of reform.[13] Although Hawthorne claimed in his preface that he would not "voluntarily have undertaken the work here offered to the public" (23: 273), he did volunteer for the job.[14] Pierce was nominated by the Democrats on the forty-ninth ballot at their convention the first week of June in 1852. The day after hearing the news Hawthorne wrote to Pierce, congratulating him on the nomination and coyly expressing his interest in the job. "It has occurred to me," he told Pierce, "that you might have some thoughts of getting me to write the necessary biography" (16: 545). He began collecting materials for the campaign biography immediately, even though he did not actually begin writing it until 25 July.

Some reviewers treated the work as if it were fiction. The *Salem Register* entitled its review "Hawthorne's New Romance," and the *Springfield Republican* called it Hawthorne's "best" fiction, revealing a "greater degree of inventive genius than any of his previous works."[15] Hawthorne himself helped promote the generic confusion by advising his publisher, Ticknor and Fields, to advertise the volume as "HAWTHORNE'S Life of GENERAL PIERCE" (16: 588), and after the fact he would admit to Horatio Bridge that, "though the story is true, yet it took a romancer to do it" (16: 605). Borrowing terms central to his fiction – the power of sympathy and the human heart – Hawthorne emphasizes Pierce's personal magnetism. "Few men possess any thing like it," Hawthorne wrote, "so irresistible as it is, so sure to draw forth an undoubting confidence, and so true to the promise which it gives" (23: 282). Characterizing Pierce's evolving relationship with the people of New Hampshire, Hawthorne observes that their "sentiment towards him soon grew to be nothing short of enthusiasm; love, pride, the sense of brotherhood, affectionate sympathy, and perfect trust, all mingled in it. It was the influence of a great heart, pervading the general heart, and throbbing with it in the same pulsation" (23: 305). Hawthorne's romance of Pierce proved successful, of course. Pierce won the 1852 election.

A month or so after the campaign biography appeared, Hawthorne commented to Longfellow that he was "beginning to take root" at the Wayside in Concord and for the first time in his life felt "really at home" (16: 602). The statement turned out to be ironic. As a benefit of his friendship with Pierce, Hawthorne was appointed American Consul in Liverpool. Hawthorne considered it his just due. Pierce "certainly owes me something," he wrote in a letter to Horatio Bridge; "for the biography has cost me hundreds of friends, here at the north . . . who drop off from me like autumn leaves, in consequence of what I say on the slavery question" (16: 605). The Hawthornes left for England on 6 July 1853, and ended up spending seven years abroad, in England (July 1853–January 1858), in Italy (January 1858–June 1859), and then again in England (June 1859–June 1860).[16]

For a man who had worried about money his entire adult life, the Liverpool consulship was a godsend for Hawthorne. His letters during his tenure include many assessments of his financial situation and worry that Congress would limit the pay of consuls. He expected to put aside $20,000 by the time he left the position.[17] Hawthorne wrote very little during his English years – except for keeping a notebook he would later use for a series of essays on England. He commented in a January 1855 letter that he had the "germ of a new romance" in his mind – apparently "The Ancestral Footstep."[18] In one of the oddest experiences of Hawthorne's life, he became involved with an American woman, Delia Bacon, who was possessed by the idea that Shakespeare did not write the plays for which he has been credited. Hawthorne eventually underwrote the cost of publishing her book on that subject and wrote a brief preface. Although originally captivated by her insights and enthusiasm, he ended up wishing he had "never meddled" with her, "nor she with me" (17: 577).[19]

Depending heavily on his French and Italian notebooks, he began his last published novel, *The Marble Faun*, in July 1858. Hawthorne first saw *The Faun* by Praxiteles in April, at the Capitoline Museum in Rome, and his notebooks include several extended descriptions of a statue that obviously fascinated him. Hawthorne had scant previous experience with sculpture, but his year in Rome immersed him in the world of American sculptors such as Hiram Powers, Harriet Hosmer, and Louisa Lander (who formed a portrait bust of Hawthorne that now resides in the Concord Free Public Library). The Hawthornes summered in Florence but returned to Rome in early fall, where Una became seriously ill with malaria, enduring a prolonged battle with the disease that lasted through the winter and spring of 1859.

The family returned to the United States in the summer of 1860. Resettling in Concord, Hawthorne tried to complete several novels, which survive as *The American Claimant* and *The Elixir of Life* manuscripts. In the spring of 1862 he and William Ticknor journeyed to Washington, DC, where he met President Abraham Lincoln at the White House. They also visited Harper's Ferry, the site three years before of John Brown's attempt to steal arms and to spark a slave revolt, and the Civil War battlefield at Manassas. The literary result of the trip was the essay, "Chiefly about War-Matters" (published in the *Atlantic*, July 1862), which included a rather unflattering description of Lincoln that Hawthorne deleted upon the advice of James T. Fields.[20] Hawthorne also wrote a second Civil War piece, entitled "Northern Volunteers" (published in the Concord *Monitor* in June 1862). Although he tried unsuccessfully to turn his English materials into a romance, he was able to write and publish a series of essays about his English experience and then collect them, along with other materials from his English notebooks, in *Our Old Home* (1863), which he dedicated to Franklin Pierce, further alienating his abolitionist friends and neighbors.

Hawthorne's health was failing, however, and on 19 May 1864, accompanying Franklin Pierce on a tour of New Hampshire, he died unexpectedly in Plymouth. Pierce was the last to see him alive and the first to report his death.

At two o'clock, I went to H's bedside; he was apparently in a sound sleep and I did not place my hand upon him. At four o'clock I went into his room again, and as his position was unchanged, I placed my hand upon him and found that life was extinct . . . He lies upon his side, his position so perfectly natural and easy, his eyes closed, that it is difficult to realize, while looking upon his noble face, that this is death.   (18: 656)

Emerson, Longfellow, and many other nineteenth-century writers attended his funeral in Concord on 21 May. Louisa May Alcott arranged the flowers (Wineapple, 378). Hawthorne was buried in Sleepy Hollow cemetery, where his body still lies directly across from Henry David Thoreau's grave and very close to Ralph Waldo Emerson's and Louisa May Alcott's on what is called "Author's Ridge."

Chapter 2

Hawthorne's contexts

Despite Hawthorne's reputation as a romancer who preferred to create a "neutral territory, somewhere between the real world and fairy-land" (1: 36) and seemed intent upon liberating his tales and novels from the everyday world, he paid careful attention to historical settings for most of his literary works. He conducted his research, often reading extensively in historical sources, but he routinely changed facts to suit his imaginative purpose. He often sought historical distance as a way of dealing with volatile contemporary issues, such as slavery or women's rights. Regardless of a work's situation in history, however, readers must deal with a tension between historical moments. *The Scarlet Letter* offers the best case in point. Set in Puritan Boston between 1642 and 1649 (the years of the English Civil War), the novel owes a great deal to seventeenth-century sources, but the most interesting recent research has emphasized the book's treatment of nineteenth-century issues. A key challenge for readers often means figuring out how Hawthorne's use of early history helps him deal with more contemporary matters.

Puritanism

Puritanism and the history of early Massachusetts settlements – Massachusetts Bay, Plymouth, and Salem – form one important context in which to understand Hawthorne's writing. Hawthorne read widely in seventeenth-century history, both English and American. Scholars such as Charles Ryskamp and Michael Colacurcio have meticulously connected characters and events in *The Scarlet Letter* and other works to the New England historical record.[1] *The Journal of John Winthrop* and Winthrop's *The History of New England from 1630 to 1649* (1825–26), Caleb H. Snow's *A History of Boston* (1825), and Joseph Felt's *The Annals of Salem from Its First Settlement* (1827) represent especially important sources from which Hawthorne took background information. He also drew upon aspects of his personal history. In both "Young Goodman Brown" and *The Scarlet Letter*, he refers to his earliest American ancestors. Hawthorne's great-great-great grandfather, William Hathorne, was a notable public figure in Salem after he settled there in 1636, serving on the Board of Selectmen for many years and fighting in King Philip's War. At one point, he ordered a Quaker woman, Ann Coleman, to be whipped through the streets of Salem. John Hathorne, William's son, presided at the Salem witch trials in 1692. In "The Custom-House," the preface he wrote to *The Scarlet Letter*, Hawthorne referred to each of these ancestors as a "bitter persecutor" who possessed "all the Puritanic traits, both good and evil" (1: 9). Hawthorne felt haunted by these ancestors and took shame upon himself "for their sakes," hoping that *The Scarlet Letter* would cause "any curse incurred by them" to be "now and henceforth removed" (1: 10).

Hawthorne's portrait of the Puritans, especially in *The Scarlet Letter*, has probably influenced our impression of Puritanism more than any other literary work, with the possible exception of Arthur Miller's treatment of the Salem witch trials in *The Crucible* (1952). That is, we associate Puritanism with superstition, excessive moralism, intolerance, and patriarchal oppression. When he describes the settlement of Puritans in "The May-Pole of Merry Mount," Hawthorne describes the inhabitants as

> dismal wretches, who said their prayers before daylight, and then wrought in the forest or the cornfield, till evening made it prayer time again. Their weapons were always at hand, to shoot down the straggling savage. When they met in conclave, it was never to keep up the old English mirth, but to hear sermons three hours long, or to proclaim bounties on the heads of wolves and the scalps of Indians. Their festivals were fast-days, and their chief pastime the singing of psalms. Woe to the youth or maiden, who did but dream of a dance! The selectman nodded to the constable; and there sat the light-heeled reprobate in the stocks; or if he danced, it was round the whipping-post, which might be termed the Puritan May-Pole.   (9: 60–61)

Many readers' impression of Puritanism is neatly captured in this passage. American Puritanism, however, was more complicated.

As a religious philosophy Puritanism was a form of Protestantism, a version of Calvinism, and strongly anti-Catholic. Puritans were dissenters, and they espoused a "purer" form of Protestantism than they saw in the Church of England in the 1630s. According to Perry Miller, the "very heart" of Puritanism was the belief in "supernatural grace," which comes upon the elect with "irresistible force and depends upon no antecedent conditions or preparations."[2] Men and women can do nothing to earn grace or to avoid it. Puritans nevertheless examined themselves and their behavior to detect signs that they were elect (chosen for salvation). The key controversy in early Puritan New England – the Antinomian controversy of 1636–38 – involved charges by Anne Hutchinson that most ministers in the Massachusetts Bay Colony were preaching a "Covenant of Works" rather than a "Covenant of Grace." By this term, David Hall explains, "she meant that the ministers were letting people 'thinke [themselves] to be saved, because they see some worke of Sanctification in them.'"[3] For Hutchinson individual behavior played no role in salvation, but she also based her ministry on a "personal sense of communion with the Holy Spirit" and so "could deny that the ministry was needed as an intervening 'means of grace' between God and man" (Hall, 18). For making charges against other ministers (all of them men) and for hosting religious services for women in her home, Hutchinson was banished to Rhode Island in 1638.

In America, Puritanism was also a utopian social philosophy. *The Scarlet Letter* deserves to be read as an American utopian novel, investigating the challenges of establishing a new society on American soil and dealing of course with the problem of dissent. The Pilgrims at Plymouth and the Puritans at Massachusetts Bay Colony (later Boston) recognized the opportunity to build a new society literally from the ground up. It would be a religious society, to be sure, a theocracy in which church and civil governments were virtually identical (at least at first). In "The May-Pole at Merry Mount" Hawthorne seems severely critical of the Puritans, especially in contrast to the free-spirited Merry Mounters, but he does represent them as such nation builders.

Puritan beliefs lay behind the Salem witchcraft hysteria of 1692, in which twenty people from Salem Village (now Danvers, Massachusetts) were executed for practicing witchcraft on their neighbors. Supporting the convictions was the belief in specter evidence – a belief that people could give Satan permission to take over their likenesses and so tempt others to sin. In fact, debate hinged on the question of whether Satan had the power to impersonate individuals without their permission, for if he did, then they could hardly be considered guilty. In the end, magistrates decided that Satan did have such power, and the persecutions of "witches" ceased. As David Levin has shown, Hawthorne treats the use of specter evidence most directly in "Young Goodman Brown," as Brown encounters the specters of virtually everyone he knows. Brown accepts them as real and judges them severely.[4]

Hawthorne also drew upon his knowledge of English history, and several of his narratives, including *The Scarlet Letter*, respond to events occurring in England. For the character of Roger Prynne (Chillingworth), Hawthorne took the last name from William Prynne (1600–69), an anti-Catholic Protestant, who strongly criticized King Charles I and Archbishop of Canterbury William Laud.[5] One of Laud's protégés, moreover, was William Chillingworth, enabling

Hawthorne to take both of his characters' names from the same historical situation. When Prynne published diatribes against Laud, whom he considered a Catholic in disguise, he was punished by having the letters "SL" (for "Seditious Libeller") burnt into his cheeks. Hawthorne must have enjoyed the coincidence of writing a story about a similar punishment that bore the same initials. Uncannily anticipating Hester's alteration of the scarlet letter and its meaning, Prynne responded to his branding by composing a two-line Latin poem, in which he interpreted the "SL" on his cheeks as *Stigmata Laudis*, the Scars of Laud.

Hester Prynne has historical sources, too, but American rather than English. In his *History of New England*, John Winthrop notes that Mary Latham of Plymouth Colony and James Britton were condemned to die for adultery in March 1644. Winthrop explains that Mary Latham had been rejected by a young man she loved, vowed to marry the "next that came to her," and ended up "matched with an ancient man" for whom she had no affection. Hawthorne also knew the case of Salem's Hester Craford, who in 1688 was ordered to be "severely whipped" for fornication with John Wedg. The judgment, which was carried out by William Hathorne, was suspended for a month so that this Hester could give birth to the child she and Wedg had conceived.

An earlier and more important antecedent is Anne Hutchinson, who was banished from Massachusetts for unlawful preaching and, in Governor John Winthrop's words, for "being a woman not fit for our society" (Hall, *The Antinomian Controversy*, 348). Hawthorne had devoted one of his earliest sketches, "Mrs. Hutchinson" (1830), to her experiences. In the first chapter of the novel Hawthorne observes that a rose bush grows by the prison door – a rose bush that had "sprung up under the foot of the sainted Ann Hutchinson" (1: 48). Hutchinson was charged with unlawfully hosting weekly meetings for women – behavior, in Winthrop's terms, not "fitting for your sex" (Hall, 312). The Puritans' objections to Hutchinson involved her interpretation of scripture, but the magistrates' comments also suggest that they resented having a woman doing that heretical preaching. In the very middle of *The Scarlet Letter* (chapter 13) Hawthorne explicitly compares Hester Prynne to Hutchinson – as a woman and a radical. If Hester had not had Pearl to keep her rooted in her family responsibilities, he says, "she might have come down to us in history, hand in hand with Ann Hutchinson, as the foundress of a religious sect. She might . . . have been a prophetess" (1: 165). By which he seems to mean a feminist, for he goes on to suggest, in terms that resonate more for nineteenth-century readers than they would have for his seventeenth-century characters, that Hester might have sponsored a movement in which the "whole system of society is to be torn down, and built up anew" so that women "can be allowed to assume what seems a fair and suitable position" (1: 165).

Transcendentalism

When Ralph Waldo Emerson published the pamphlet *Nature* in 1836, most scholars agree, the so-called Transcendentalist movement began. Part religious movement, part social movement, part aesthetic movement, Transcendentalism proves difficult to define. Insofar as Emerson was its leading representative, it can be described as an American form of idealism and Romanticism. Placing the individual self at the center of experience, even religious experience, Transcendentalists emphasized the direct experience of God, usually through nature. "Let me admonish you, first of all, to go alone," Emerson advised the Harvard Divinity School graduating class in 1838; "to refuse the good models, even those which are sacred in the imagination of men, and dare to love God without mediator or veil."[6] A key Transcendentalist trope was transparency – registering a belief that the human mind could see through appearances to a "real" reality underneath. The most famous example occurs in *Nature*, when Emerson describes a spiritual and imaginative epiphany:

> In the woods too, a man casts off his years, as the snake his slough, and what period soever of life, is always a child. In the woods is perpetual youth . . . There I feel that nothing can befall me in life, – no disgrace, no calamity, (leaving me my eyes,) which nature cannot repair. Standing on the bare ground, – my head bathed by the blithe air, and uplifted into infinite space, – all mean egotism vanishes. I become a transparent eye-ball. I am nothing. I see all. The currents of the Universal Being circulate through me; I am part or particle of God.   (*Nature*, 10)

Emerson posits the possibility of perfect vision that renders the world transparent so that the visionary can see through to the world of Ideas.

Although without a formal organizational structure, Transcendentalism offered an umbrella for many social reform movements, including abolitionism, women's rights, educational reform, and utopian experimentation. Here, too, the key principle involved celebrating individual freedom. "To believe your own thought, to believe that what is true for you in your private heart, is true for all men; that is genius," Emerson wrote in "Self-Reliance" (1841).[7] As an aesthetic or literary movement, it contributed most notably to Thoreau's *Walden* (1854) and to Walt Whitman's *Leaves of Grass* (1855). "Each age, it is found, must write its own books," Emerson wrote in "The American Scholar," a literary declaration of independence.[8]

Hawthorne had an uncomfortable relationship with Transcendentalism. Part of it was personal. As Larry Reynolds notes, when Hawthorne moved to Concord after his marriage to Sophia Peabody in 1842, he "entered an Emersonian world, which inspired and challenged him. Emerson had preceded Hawthorne in his new house, the Manse, in the affections of his wife, Sophia, and in the natural setting he now found so appealing."[9] Hawthorne depicted Emerson as a "mystic, stretching his hand out of cloud-land, in vain search for something real" (8: 336). In "The Old Manse," the preface he wrote for *Mosses from an Old Manse*, he devoted a lengthy section to Emerson, and he seemed especially dismissive. Characterizing Emerson's almost mesmerical influence on others, Hawthorne wrote,

> His mind acted upon other minds, of a certain constitution, with wonderful magnetism, and drew many men upon long pilgrimages, to speak with him face to face . . . Uncertain, troubled, earnest wanderers, through the midnight of the moral world, beheld his intellectual fire, as a beacon burning on a hill-top, and, climbing the difficult ascent, looked forth into the surrounding obscurity, more hopefully than hitherto. The light revealed objects unseen before – mountains, gleaming lakes, glimpses of a creation among the chaos – but also, as was unavoidable, it attracted bats and owls, and the whole host of night-birds, which flapped their dusky wings against the gazer's eyes, and sometimes were mistaken for fowls of angelic feather. Such delusions always hover nigh, whenever a beacon-fire of truth is kindled. (10: 30–31)

Toward the end of this passage, Emerson seems to be the leader of a cult following. Without directly criticizing him or his ideas, Hawthorne makes him guilty by association. Emerson is known by the quality of the people he attracts. "Never was a poor little country village infested with such a variety of queer, strangely dressed, oddly behaved mortals, most of whom took upon themselves to be important agents of the world's destiny, yet were simply bores of a very intense water" (10: 31–32).

Transcendentalism itself seemed too dreamy and optimistic to Hawthorne, and he critiqued a deformed idealism and its potentially harmful consequences in such tales as "The Birth-mark" and "Rappaccini's Daughter." "The Artist of the Beautiful" seems more ambiguous, as Owen Warland sees his beautiful mechanical butterfly crushed before his eyes. But Hawthorne concludes the story with the observation that, "when the artist rose high enough to achieve the Beautiful, the symbol by which he made it perceptible to mortal senses became of little value in his eyes, while his spirit possessed itself in the enjoyment of the Reality" (10: 475).

On a personal level, Hawthorne liked Thoreau, but he consistently distinguished Thoreau's best qualities from any taint of Transcendentalism. "In the Dial for July," Hawthorne wrote Epes Sargent in October 1842, "there is an article on the Natural History of this part of the country, which will give you an idea of him as a genuine and exquisite observer of nature." While noting that Thoreau is "somewhat tinctured with Transcendentalism," Hawthorne felt confident that he could be "a very valuable contributor" to Sargent's magazine (15: 656). Insofar as he could distance Thoreau from Transcendentalism, as Hawthorne conceived of it, he could appreciate and even envy Thoreau's idiosyncrasies. Later, when Hawthorne was serving as US Consul in Liverpool, he wrote to his publisher, William Ticknor, asking for a half dozen books he could give an English friend who wanted to read some "good American books." Of the five he requested, two were by Thoreau – *A Week on the Concord and Merrimack Rivers* and *Walden*. "You understand," Hawthorne cautioned, "that these books must not be merely good, but must be original, with American characteristics, and not generally known in England" (17: 261). The choice of Thoreau's two books is striking. Most people today would see them as central to our understanding of Transcendentalism, but Hawthorne emphasized Thoreau's naturalism in the letter he wrote Richard Monckton Milnes, when he forwarded the books. "'Walden' and 'Concord River,' are by a very remarkable man," he said, "but I hardly hope you will read his books, unless for the observation of nature contained in them" (17: 277). When Milnes wrote back, asking for more information about Thoreau, Hawthorne's response is more equivocal. Although he would as always praise Thoreau's Indian-like qualities, Hawthorne also noted that he "despises the world, and all that it has to offer, and, like other humorists, is an intolerable bore." Thoreau is an "upright, conscientious, and courageous man" of the "highest integrity," Hawthorne concluded, but "he is not an agreeable person; and in his presence one feels ashamed of having any money, or a house to live in, or so much as two coats to wear, or having written a book that the public read" (17: 279–80). Many readers, of course, have had this same reaction as they read *Walden*. Indeed, provoking his readers in order to wake them up comprised a large part of Thoreau's purpose. The last thing he wanted to be, it seems, was an "agreeable" person. Hawthorne's comment expresses common exasperation with someone he obviously respected and admired. And he clearly got Thoreau's message about materialism and economical living – a message that would have irritated the Hawthorne who had spent his life struggling to make money and usually failing to do so.

Feminism and scribbling women

Hawthorne wrote during a period of political turmoil, especially because of the human rights movements that characterize the middle of the nineteenth century. Congress passed the Indian Removal Act in 1830, giving the United

States government the authority to remove American Indians from their tribal lands. Agitation in the north over slavery heated up at the same time, with the publication of such abolitionist newspapers as William Lloyd Garrison's *The Liberator* in 1831, the same year that Nat Turner led a group of slaves on a two-day rebellion in Southampton, Virginia. In 1837, the year that Hawthorne published *Twice-Told Tales*, Mary Lyon opened Mount Holyoke Female Seminary (now Mount Holyoke College), the first institution founded to provide higher education to women. Many abolitionists argued in behalf of women's rights – for example, Lydia Maria Child in her *History of the Condition of Women* (1835), Sarah Grimké in *Letters on the Equality of the Sexes* (1838), and especially Margaret Fuller in "The Great Lawsuit" (1843) and *Woman in the Nineteenth Century*, which she published in 1845, the year before Hawthorne published *Mosses from an Old Manse*.

Hawthorne seemed minimally affected by these movements, and it was common in criticism before the last twenty years to situate his writing within a romance tradition in which "real world" concerns had only a faint presence. More recent scholars have found plenty of evidence that Hawthorne's writing bears traces of the cultural moment out of which he wrote.[10] By the time he published *The Scarlet Letter*, for example, Hawthorne knew Fuller very well. The first major women's rights convention, held in July of 1848 in Seneca Falls, New York, occurred just a year before he sat down to begin the novel about a woman who rebels against patriarchal authority. Despite the distant setting, it is hard to imagine *The Scarlet Letter* not entering into a conversation with nineteenth-century feminism.[11]

Recent scholarship on Hawthorne's writing in a context formed by women, women's issues, and women's writing, has come a long way from the character typology approaches of earlier periods. Along with James Fenimore Cooper, Edgar Allan Poe, Melville, and others, Hawthorne comes to mind when we think of nineteenth-century female stereotypes, especially the familiar opposition of Fair Maidens and Dark Ladies.[12] Cooper's Alice and Cora Munro in *The Last of the Mohicans* (1826) and Hetty and Judith Hutter in *The Deerslayer* (1841), Poe's Rowena and Ligeia in "Ligeia" (1838), Melville's Yilla and Hautia in *Mardi* (1849) and Lucy Tartan and Isabel Banford in *Pierre; or, The Ambiguities* (1852) compare with Hawthorne's Priscilla and Zenobia in *The Blithedale Romance* (1852) and Hilda and Miriam in *The Marble Faun* (1860).

Hawthorne understood the power of radical women, and in Hester Prynne, as in Anne Hutchinson, he created a heroine who is as much a nineteenth-century feminist as a seventeenth-century Puritan heretic. Zenobia in *The Blithedale Romance* is more obviously patterned after Margaret Fuller. Thomas Mitchell finds Fuller's influence pervasive, and *The Scarlet Letter* includes several passages that seem to echo lines in Fuller's ground-breaking feminist book, *Woman in the Nineteenth Century*. At the end of *The Scarlet Letter*, for example, Hester assures the women who come to her cottage of "her firm belief, that, at some brighter period, when the world should have grown ripe for it, in Heaven's own time, a new truth would be revealed, in order to establish the whole relation between man and woman on a surer ground of mutual happiness" (1: 263). When Fuller comments on the prospects for feminist reform, she writes, "then and only then will mankind be ripe for this, when inward and outward freedom for Woman as much as for Man shall be acknowledged as a *right*, not yielded as a concession" (*Woman*, 20). The unusual word "ripe" stands out in each passage; Hawthorne's use of the word in a sentence that echoes Fuller's in other respects as well suggests that he was borrowing from Fuller. Both writers look forward to a time when American society will be "ripe" for the growth of real women, and both find it very difficult to specify that time.

Hawthorne's most notorious comment about women writers occurred in a letter he wrote to his publisher, William Ticknor, in 1855, while he was serving as American Consul in Liverpool. "America is now wholly given over to a d—d mob of scribbling women, and I should have no chance of success while the public is occupied with their trash – and should be ashamed of myself if I did succeed" (17: 304). The "damned mob of scribbling women" phrase has haunted Hawthorne scholarship for many years and has led many feminist scholars to dismiss Hawthorne as a writer who had little sympathy for women's interests or feminist causes.

Hawthorne did not exactly recant his view of "scribbling women" when he wrote Ticknor two weeks later, but he did qualify his blanket indictment of women writers by making an exception for Fanny Fern and *Ruth Hall*, her powerful 1855 novella about a single mother who resorts to writing to support her family (after her husband's untimely death). "I have since been reading 'Ruth Hall,'" he wrote Ticknor, "and I must say I enjoyed it a great deal. The woman writes as if the devil was in her, and that is the only condition under which a woman ever writes anything worth reading. Generally, women write like emasculated men, and are only to be distinguished from male authors by greater feebleness and folly; but when they throw off the restraints of decency, and come before the public stark naked, as it were – then their books are sure to possess character and value" (17: 308). It would take an essay to unpack all of the implications of Hawthorne's suggestive language. In general, he doesn't like women's writing because women write like "emasculated men." But the women's writing he does like conjures up images of women writing "stark naked" (but also as if possessed by the devil).

Despite his disparagement of most women writers, Hawthorne populated his fiction with many powerful female artists. Hester Prynne is not a writer, except in the loosest sense, but she is an artist, and she comes before the public, in a sense, "stark naked." She embroiders the scarlet letter as if the Devil were in her before displaying it to the public for the first time and so asserts some power over the letter as a signifier. For the rest of the novel, her artistry seems confined to the domestic sphere, although even there it is not without its subversive power. Zenobia in *The Blithedale Romance* is a writer and noted speaker. The name "Zenobia" is a pseudonym, her "magazine-signature" (3: 13), although Coverdale disparages the "poor little stories and tracts" she publishes because they "never half did justice to her intellect" (3: 44). She was made for a "stump-oratress," he says, acknowledging the power of her personal presence and her voice. Miriam Schaefer in *The Marble Faun* is a painter, and her paintings are powerful. One depicts Jael driving a nail through the temple of Sisera (4: 43). Another shows Judith just after she has cut off the head of Holofernes. A third represents the daughter of Herodias, receiving the head of John the Baptist on a platter. "Over and over again," the narrator observes, "there was the idea of woman, acting the part of a revengeful mischief towards man" (4: 44). Miriam paints as if the Devil were in her, though one thinks that it would not be comfortable being that Devil.

Race, slavery, and abolition

Hawthorne's friendship with Franklin Pierce and his refusal to support abolition have vexed Hawthorne scholars, although no more than they vexed many of his contemporaries. Scholars invariably cite a passage from the Pierce biography in order to exemplify the conservatism of Hawthorne's thinking:

> Those Northern men, therefore, who deem the great cause of human welfare all represented and involved in this present hostility against Southern institutions – and who conceive that the world stands still, except so far as that goes forward – these, it may be allowed, can scarcely give their sympathy or their confidence to the subject of this memoir. But there is still another view, and probably as wise a one. It looks upon Slavery as one of those evils, which Divine Providence does not leave to be remedied by human contrivances, but which, in its own good time, by some means impossible to be anticipated, but of the simplest and easiest operation, when all its uses shall have been fulfilled, it causes to vanish like a dream. (23: 352)

The context of this passage, of course, is the election of 1852, the first presidential election to follow the infamous Compromise of 1850, which so enraged northerners because it reinforced the rights of slave owners to pursue fugitive slaves into free territory, arrest them, and return them to slavery. The law also made it illegal for anyone to interfere in this process; indeed, it required people in the north to aid and abet the capture of fugitive slaves. That neither Pierce nor Hawthorne was enraged angered Hawthorne's abolitionist contemporaries.

Hawthorne anticipates the explanation for Pierce's opposition to abolition at the end of *The Scarlet Letter*. Although his subject is women's rights, his logic is the same – significant social change will occur of its own accord, gradually, and in its own time. When women visit Hester's cottage, "demanding why they were so wretched, and what the remedy," she "comforted them and counselled them, as best she might":

> She assured them, too, of her firm belief, that, at some brighter period, when the world should have grown ripe for it, in Heaven's own time, a new truth would be revealed, in order to establish the whole relation between man and woman on a surer ground of mutual happiness.
>
> (1: 263)

Small consolation to those living in the present, Hawthorne's indefinite postponement of redress and almost fatalistic sense that social activism is pointless seem naively incompatible with the political activism on human rights issues that has characterized the long aftermath of the period in which he wrote.

Hawthorne rarely wrote about race or slavery or abolition in his fiction, but that has not prevented many critics from placing his writing into conversation with such important issues. Toni Morrison issued a tacit challenge to literary scholars that many have accepted:

> Explicit or implicit, the Africanist presence informs in compelling and inescapable ways the texture of American literature. It is a dark and abiding presence, there for the literary imagination as both a visible and an invisible mediating force. Even, and especially, when American texts are not "about" Africanist presences or characters or narrative or idiom, the shadow hovers in implication, in sign, in line of demarcation.[13]

The Scarlet Letter has increasingly been examined in its nineteenth-century context, and its participation in a conversation about slavery and abolition has become almost axiomatic. Critics such as Jonathan Arac and Sacvan Bercovitch have revealed Hawthorne's historicism in order to confirm his conservatism – his failure to oppose slavery and embrace abolition. Arguing that Hester's scarlet A resembles the United States Constitution as a contested text, Arac considers the "indeterminacy" of the letter's meaning a strategy on Hawthorne's part for avoiding political action and change. *The Scarlet Letter*, he believes, is "propaganda – *not* to change your life."[14] Bercovitch also considers *The Scarlet Letter* to be "thick propaganda," and he cites Hawthorne's "ironies of reconciliation" and laissez-faire "strategy of inaction" as key ingredients in the liberal ideology that sponsored numerous compromises with slavery, especially in 1850, the year of *The Scarlet Letter*'s publication.[15]

Jean Fagan Yellin has gone furthest in exploring the novel's inscription by slavery and abolitionist discourses and convincingly established Hawthorne's knowledge of anti-slavery feminism. She has linked Hester iconographically to female slaves as sisters in bondage even as she stresses Hawthorne's refusal to let Hester function as a full-fledged anti-slavery feminist.[16] "*The Scarlet Letter* presents a classic displacement," Yellin points out: "color is the sign not of race, but of grace – and of its absence. Black skin is seen as blackened soul." When "'black' is read as describing skin color and not moral status, the text of *The Scarlet Letter* reveals the obsessive concern with blacks and blackness, with the presence of a dangerous dark group within society's midst, that is characteristic of American political discourse in the last decades before Emancipation."[17]

More recently, scholars such as Brenda Wineapple and Larry Reynolds have provided more balanced assessments of Hawthorne's attitudes toward race and slavery – acknowledging his opposition to abolition and even his racism, while seeking to understand his attitudes within both biographical and cultural contexts. Wineapple has carefully researched Nathaniel and Sophia Hawthorne's racial attitudes, and she provides plenty of evidence to link Hawthorne with views that contemporary readers find repugnant. The Hawthornes' racism, however, makes them typical rather than exceptional within their New England peer group. Most provocatively, Wineapple quotes from a letter Sophia wrote to her sister, Mary Peabody Mann in 1848. The Hawthornes had been invited for dinner, and at the table was Chloe Lee, an African American student who was boarding with the Manns. Sophia later "protested." "I could scarcely eat my supper, so intolerable was the odor wafting from her to me" (*Hawthorne*, 199). We are very close to a truly appalling portrait of Hawthorne, even though Wineapple is careful not to identify Hawthorne with Sophia's racism.

In a notebook entry from 1850, on the other hand, Hawthorne betrays his racial prejudice when he records his attendance at the National Theatre for a pantomime of "Jack the Giant Killer." Devoting his attention to the crowd, he describes two young women, one of whom – "a large, plump girl" – is wearing the "vilest gown" of "dirty white cotton, so pervadingly dingy that it was white no longer." It was the "shabbiest and dirtiest dress, in a word, that I ever saw a woman wear" (8: 502). Hawthorne's imagination moves quickly from color to race. The dirty, formerly white dress leads him to note the woman's dark complexion – "so dark that I rather suspected her to have a tinge of African blood" (8: 503). David Anthony cites this passage in order to analyze how Hawthorne's anxieties in a situation where he feels out of place focus on color and racial difference.[18]

Wineapple recognizes the tissue of political beliefs and prejudices that produced Hawthorne's politics – and his racism: his skepticism about all reform movements, a belief in states' rights that prompted him to sign a petition protesting the Fugitive Slave Law, his agreement with college friend and benefactor Horatio Bridge in supporting colonization (187). Hawthorne despised the slave trade and did not support slavery, but he wouldn't go the next step and support abolition. He did seem exercised, like so many others, about the Fugitive Slave Law, however – commenting to Longfellow in an 8 May 1851 letter that the law "is the only thing that could have blown me into any respectable degree on this great subject of the day" (16: 431). Hawthorne could not see slavery as an absolute evil – only a relative one. He believed that conditions would worsen not improve for freed slaves. He also believed that slavery would vanish naturally. Today, we don't accept this vision as one that a reasonable man could hold – not even in the middle of the nineteenth century, not even when many other people held it.

Larry Reynolds attributes Hawthorne's opposition to abolitionism, however, to his lifelong social and political conservatism and his persistent fear of fanaticism and "radical sociopolitical behavior."[19] While most of his New England contemporaries shared those views initially, many of them accepted more radical ideas in the run-up to the Civil War – condoning violence, such as John Brown's, in the service of abolitionism (Reynolds, 50–51). Hawthorne did not change during the antebellum period, and like his friend Franklin Pierce, he consistently supported preservation of the Union, fearing any violence that would tear the Union apart. In his final assessment, Reynolds credits Hawthorne with possessing a "politics of imagination," which "allowed him to resist the kind of groupthink leading to violence and death" (64).

After he returned to America in 1860 and experienced the beginning and early years of the Civil War, Hawthorne sounded every bit a pro-northern, anti-slavery, anti-south partisan. He did worry more than many that the north's goals were not clear, and some of his observations seem prophetic. "If we pummel the South ever so hard," he wrote Bridge, shortly after the war began (26 May 1861), "they will love us none the better for it." But Hawthorne agreed that abolishing slavery in the south was a worthy goal. "If we are fighting for the annihilation of slavery, to be sure, it may be a wise object, and offers a tangible result, and the only one which is consistent with a future Union between North and South" (18: 381). In the campaign biography Hawthorne had used the need to preserve the Union as Pierce's reason for opposing immediate abolition of slavery. He had changed his mind in 1861. "If we stop fighting at this juncture," he told an English friend, "we give up Maryland, Virginia, Kentucky, Missouri, all of which are fully capable of being made free-soil, and will be so in a few years, if we possess them, but not in a hundred years, if we lose them" (18: 420). Indeed, he repeatedly suggested that the North cast off at least some of the southern states in order to form a new Union. "I trust we shall cast off the extreme southern states," he argued, "and giving them a parting kick, let them go to perdition in their own way. I want no more of their territory than we can digest into free soil" (18: 421). Like a lot of northerners, Hawthorne would tire of a war that most thought would be brief. By March of 1863, he had lost his enthusiasm for the fight, and he was ready for New England to become a "nation by itself" (18: 543).

Hawthorne tested his thinking in a lengthy letter (July 1863) to his sister-in-law, Elizabeth Peabody, an ardent abolitionist with whom he had clashed several times. He distanced himself from the "Peace Democrats," who were willing to end the war and restore the Union to its antebellum condition (with slavery in place in the south). "You cannot possibly conceive (looking through spectacles of the tint which yours have acquired) how little the North really cares for the Negro-question, and how eagerly it would grasp at peace if recommended by a delusive show of victory. Free soil was never in so great danger as now" (18: 591). Although Hawthorne himself was frequently accused of being a Copperhead, or Peace Democrat, like Pierce, the views he expresses to Peabody seem quite different. Hawthorne warns her about the dangers of settling for peace at any cost, citing a lack of commitment among many northerners to the full eradication of slavery.

Hawthorne found it virtually impossible to write fiction – romances – during the war, but he did make a serious effort to connect his writing to current events. He visited Washington, DC, along with Harper's Ferry and the Manassas battlefield. He wrote and published two Civil War essays, "Chiefly about War Matters" and "Northern Volunteers." The former essay includes a description of a group of fugitive slaves whom Hawthorne encountered on the road, "escaping out of the mysterious depths of Secessia." "They were unlike the specimens of the race whom we are accustomed to see at the North," he observed, "and, in my judgment, were far more agreeable" (23: 419). As Nancy Bentley has pointed out, one of the reasons these contrabands appear more agreeable is that Hawthorne can adapt them to the primitivist model he had employed in *The Marble Faun* to describe the faun-like Donatello.[20] They are "so picturesquely natural in manners," he notes, "and wearing such a crust of primeval simplicity, (which is quite polished away from the northern black man,) that they seemed a kind of creature by themselves, not altogether human, but perhaps quite as good, and akin to the fauns and rustic deities of olden times" (23: 420). Hawthorne goes on, however, in terms that would provoke outrage in William Lloyd Garrison, to say that, while he feels kingly toward the "poor fugitives," he doesn't know what to hope for on their behalf. He wonders if they will be better off in the north, although he would not have them turned back, and he concludes with the insight that, "whoever may be benefitted by the results of this war, it will not be the present generation of negroes, the childhood of whose race is now gone forever, and who must henceforth fight a hard battle with the world, on very unequal terms" (23: 420).[21]

Nineteenth-century manhood

The nineteenth century marked significant changes in conceptions of manhood and womanhood. Michael Kimmel notes that at the beginning of the century American manhood was "rooted in landownership (the Genteel Patriarch) or in the self-possession of the independent artisan, shopkeeper, or farmer (the Heroic Artisan)." During the 1800s, thanks to the Industrial Revolution, paradigms shifted, and "American men began to link their sense of themselves as men to their position in the volatile marketplace, to their economic success – a far less stable yet far more exciting and potentially rewarding peg upon which to hang one's identity. The Self-Made Man of American mythology was born anxious and insecure."[22] As T. Walter Herbert notes, Hawthorne "lived out the classic story of masculine success in America, overcoming early hardship to achieve wealth and fame"; "yet a desolating sense of unreality plagued" him throughout his life. He "was sharply aware that the reigning model of manhood, defined by unceasing self-reliant competition, violated his own native temperament."[23]

Hawthorne wrote as more and more women were taking up the pen and earning money for their labors. Harriet Beecher Stowe published *Uncle Tom's Cabin* in 1852, the same year that Hawthorne published *The Blithedale Romance*. Stowe's book sold more than 300,000 copies in its first year. Hawthorne's *The Scarlet Letter*, by far his best-selling book up to that point in his career (1850), went through three editions and sold a respectable 6,000 copies in its first year. *Uncle Tom's Cabin* sold that many the first day it was available.[24] Writing remained a respectable occupation for men, as well as for women, but other occupations, especially in business and industry, increasingly became associated with manliness in a way that authorship did not.

It seems appropriate to situate Hawthorne within the context of changing conceptions of manhood. Hawthorne remained a bachelor until he was thirty-eight years old at a time when the male purity movement focused attention on the dangers of male narcissism. The well-known separation of men's and women's occupations into different spheres – the home for women, the workplace outside the home for men – also changed conceptions of parenting and fatherhood at the very time that Hawthorne became a father.

We don't usually think of Hawthorne as a working man, but it is interesting to place him in the company of other laborers. In 1851 Hawthorne wrote to his friend and fellow Custom House officer, Zachariah Burchmore, two years after the two of them had been sacked from their jobs: "I have not, as you suggest, the slightest sympathy for the slaves, or, at least, not half so much as for the laboring whites, who, I believe, as a general thing, are ten times worse off than the Southern negroes" (16: 456). Here again, of course, Hawthorne fails to sympathize with slaves and with people he calls "Southern Negroes." He does express sympathy for the plight of northern laborers, a group in which he may have numbered himself.

The question of gender identity looms especially large when we situate Hawthorne in the world of work. There are many references to Hawthorne's feminine qualities. Wineapple quotes one of his Bowdoin classmates, who described him as "shrinking almost like a girl from all general intercourse either in the sports or meetings of his fellow students" (*Hawthorne* 50). Margaret Fuller concluded that "The Gentle Boy" possessed "so much grace and delicacy of feeling" that it "must have been written by a woman," and Henry Wadsworth Longfellow commented that Hawthorne's "genius" included "a large proportion of feminine elements."[25] Hawthorne bristled at such characterizations, even though, in taking up storytelling as his life's work, as Wineapple observes, he knew that he had taken up "a kind of women's work, decorative and useless, an idler's trade, not a manly one" (78–79).

Hawthorne's identification with "laboring whites," therefore, is intriguing – less because of the racial modifier than because of the socio-economic class angle. Wineapple pursues this identification when she discusses Hawthorne's stint as measurer in the Boston Custom House (1839–41). Hawthorne "held on to his government job not just because he needed the money or because the country ignored its artists – though both were true – but because he liked it." "He felt rejuvenated at the docks: the bustle, the sheer movement of men, or the looping of the gulls and, below, the dark ships' bellies, where the coal was stowed. All this brought him close to the young clerks and laborers who sweated at real jobs for quantifiable results" (133). Wineapple's portrait of Hawthorne differs markedly from Walter Herbert's. Citing early Hawthorne letters – the one in which Hawthorne wonders why he wasn't a girl so that he could be "pinned" all his life to his "Mother's apron" (15: 117) and the college letter in which he wishes that he might be "rich enough to live without a profession" (15: 139) – Herbert observes that "this sounds very remote from the ethos of manly striving that was taking form in the culture at large. Instead of welcoming the contest among democratic equals, young Hawthorne yearns for a seclusion that is both girlish and aristocratic."[26] Hawthorne suffered for much of his adult life from career anxiety – like the perpetual student who can't find or keep a steady job, and lives at home periodically in the process.

His belated identification with other workers – partly a feeling of class solidarity, partly compensation for his scribbling – makes Hawthorne's decision to join the Brook Farm utopian community more understandable. Life at Brook Farm promised the perfect combination of hard physical and mental labor. "The union of thinker and worker," Wineapple notes, "was irresistible to a man whose conscience still carped about idleness and still considered writing a frivolous pastime . . . Hoeing and milking and feeding and mulching are honest occupations, chores performed in the cowhide boots of a democratic manhood" (147). As his letters and notebooks show, Hawthorne liked this sort of work, at least for a while and up to a point – the point where he discovered that he was spending more time shoveling manure than writing. Placed within a context of work at a time when writing for men like Hawthorne really was day labor and piece work, this working-class Hawthorne contrasts with most characterizations of him and the men of his fiction.

When we think of Hawthorne's most notable male characters, we see a common type predominate. Arthur Dimmesdale, Miles Coverdale, and Kenyon in the novels, Robin Molineux, Reuben Bourne, Reverend Hooper, Wakefield, Goodman Brown, Owen Warland, Giovanni Guasconti in the tales – none of these male characters would evoke an image of traditional manliness in either nineteenth- or twentieth-century terms. They differ from one another, to be sure, but even when plotted along a range of masculinity, they group toward one end of the spectrum. Characterized by relative physical slightness and weakness, they are pale, tremulous, but sensitive – artistic types, who, like Hawthorne himself, are shy and a little mysterious. They are more feminine than masculine – but handsome – a lot like Hawthorne himself.

Chapter 3

Hawthorne's short fiction

Besides five novels (*Fanshawe, The Scarlet Letter, The House of the Seven Gables, The Blithedale Romance*, and *The Marble Faun*), Hawthorne published three collections of tales (*Twice-Told Tales, Mosses from an Old Manse*, and *The Snow-Image*), from which contemporary readers probably know about a dozen stories. Hawthorne had an unusual career, in fact, for a writer whom many consider the greatest American writer of the nineteenth century. Except for the early novel (*Fanshawe*) that he disavowed and tried to suppress,[1] he wrote only short stories and sketches for the first twenty years of his career. Then, in 1850 (at the age of 45), he published *The Scarlet Letter* – a novel, and the longest, most complex work he had yet published. After that, he wrote virtually no short fiction for the rest of his career. Instead, he wrote additional long works.

Hawthorne labeled those long works romances rather than novels, and the distinction he made has influenced scholars looking for ways to define an American tradition of novel writing. In his preface ("The Custom-House") to *The Scarlet Letter, a Romance* (its full title), he noted that "moonlight, in a familiar room, falling so white upon the carpet, and showing its figures so distinctly, – making every object so minutely visible, yet so unlike a morning or noontide visibility, – is a medium the most suitable for a romance-writer" (1: 35). Hawthorne means that his work is not quite realistic, if that means shining the brightest and most clarifying light upon details in the daily world we all know. He will use familiar objects, but reflect them in the slightly distorting light of the moon. In preferring night light to daylight, Hawthorne implies that his fiction may express the truths of dreams or even nightmares. Objects will be "so spiritualized by the unusual light, that they seem to lose their actual substance, and become things of intellect" (1: 35). In his most famous figure, Hawthorne concludes that, under these conditions, "the floor of our familiar room has become a neutral territory, somewhere between the real world and fairy-land, where the Actual and Imaginary may meet, and each imbue itself with the nature of the other" (1: 36).

In his preface to *The House of the Seven Gables,* Hawthorne makes the distinction between novels and romances even sharper. He opens the preface by writing:

> When a writer calls his work a Romance, it need hardly be observed that he wishes to claim a certain latitude, both as to its fashion and material, which he would not have felt himself entitled to assume, had he professed to be writing a Novel. The latter form of composition is presumed to aim at a very minute fidelity, not merely to the possible, but to the probable and ordinary course of man's experience. The former – while, as a work of art, it must rigidly subject itself to laws, and while it sins unpardonably, so far as it may swerve aside from the truth of the human heart – has fairly a right to present that truth under circumstances, to a great extent, of the writer's own choosing or creation. If he think fit, also, he may so manage his atmospherical medium as to bring out or mellow the lights and deepen and enrich the shadows of the picture. He will be wise, no doubt, to mingle the Marvellous rather as a slight, delicate, and evanescent flavor, than as any portion of the actual substance of the dish offered to the Public. He can hardly be said, however, to commit a literary crime, even if he disregard this caution.   (2: 1)

Hawthorne claims a lot of poetic license for himself in this passage, so long as he faithfully represents the "truth of the human heart." In grounding his sense of truth in the heart rather than in the mind, Hawthorne invokes the power of feelings more than reason or thought. We know how much powerful feelings can distort our thinking and even our perception of objects and other people. It is not surprising that so many readers have brought the insights of psychological and psychoanalytic analysis to bear upon Hawthorne's writing.

Hawthorne did not develop his theory of Romance only when he started to write long works, such as *The Scarlet Letter.* As I noted, he wrote short stories and sketches for the first two decades of his career, and those short works lay the groundwork for the longer works that follow. Hawthorne struggled during the first decade of his career, even though he wrote and published numerous tales – all of them anonymously. He tried unsuccessfully to find a publisher for three different collections of tales, before finally publishing *Twice-Told Tales* in 1837. Even so, he must have learned valuable lessons about the type of collection he should put together, because he carefully edited the tales he included in *Twice-Told Tales* with his audience in mind, making "numerous changes which reveal his sensitivity to current, often prudish, standards of taste," Donald Crowley observes. Wanting to "avoid any matter his audience might consider prurient," he demonstrated that "his acute sense of the limitations of his readers made him unwilling to risk printing in acknowledged tales some words and attitudes he had felt free to publish anonymously."[2] Hawthorne's "acute sense" of his readers and their limitations must also have governed his decisions about the volume as a whole. By the time the first collection was published, he had about four dozen tales and sketches from which to choose. *Twice-Told Tales* included eighteen, so Hawthorne excluded more than two dozen tales from the book, including many we now consider Hawthorne's best – "Roger Malvin's Burial," "Young Goodman Brown," "Alice Doane's Appeal," and "My Kinsman, Major Molineux." Of the tales collected in that first volume, "The Gentle Boy" was the most popular during Hawthorne's lifetime, while stories such as "Wakefield," "The Gray Champion," "The May-Pole of Merry Mount," and "The Minister's Black Veil" have become more popular among modern readers.

Arguably, the most important single reader-response Hawthorne received was not Melville's belated notice of *Mosses from an Old Manse* in 1850, but Henry Wadsworth Longfellow's review of the 1837 *Twice-Told Tales*. Longfellow wrote Hawthorne that "what most delighted" him in the tales was "the simple representation of what may be called small-life."[3] Longfellow's review follows in the same vein. These tales and sketches, he asserts, "have been gathered fresh from the secret places of a peaceful and gentle heart . . . The book, though in prose, is written nevertheless by a poet. He looks upon all things in the spirit of love, and with lively sympathies." Longfellow considers *Twice-Told Tales* a "'sweet, sweet book.'"[4] If his Hawthorne does not much resemble our own, or the "dark" Hawthorne whom Melville would later praise, the reason lies in the choices Hawthorne himself made for *Twice-Told Tales*.

Hawthorne's first collection did not include only light-hearted tales. If one of his goals was to appeal to the women readers who were becoming an increasingly important audience for fiction, he made some odd choices. Negative representations of marriage, family, and the whole domestic sphere haunt so many of these early tales that they constitute a leitmotif of gothic fear and horror. "The Hollow of the Three Hills" (1830), for example, sketches out a chilling paradigm of domestic trouble in the auditory "visions" an old crone grants an estranged woman. Her mother and father speak of a daughter "bearing dishonor along with her, and leaving shame and affliction to bring their gray heads to the grave" (10: 202). Her husband talks of "woman's perfidy, of a wife who had broken her holiest vows, of a home and heart made desolate" (10: 203). Finally, the woman witnesses her own funeral procession and hears the "revilings and anathemas, whispered but distinct, from women and from men, breathed against the daughter who had wrung the aged hearts of her parents, – the wife who had betrayed the trusting fondness of her husband, – the mother who had sinned against natural affection, and left her child to die"

(10: 204). In varying degrees, Hawthorne's early fiction repeats such visions of estrangement, betrayal, bad parenting, and other domestic evils.

"Alice Doane's Appeal"

Hawthorne imagines women's roles far removed from the "cult of true womanhood" then emerging in the nineteenth century and founded on "four cardinal virtues – piety, purity, submissiveness and domesticity."[5] In a recently published essay on Hawthorne's early tales, I examined Hawthorne's efforts to work out his authorial relationship to potential female readers by examining the ways in which he seems to be manipulating female characters and in turn the readers who identify with them.[6] "Alice Doane's Appeal" provides an especially good example, as Hawthorne dramatizes his rhetorical relationship to female readers in the relationship between his narrator and the two women he escorts to Gallows Hill in Salem, the scene of the witches' executions. He explores his narrator's success and failure in controlling the responses of these two female listeners. The tale offers an object lesson in author–audience relations and especially in the male artist's power over female response. After leading the two young women to the top of Gallows Hill, the narrator hopes to exploit their "feminine susceptibility," the tendency of their emotions to come and go with "quick vicissitude" (11: 268). Through the relationship he stages between these two female "readers" and his male narrator, Hawthorne analyzes the writing process dynamically – as if measuring the impact on a focus group of two. As Christopher Packard observes, the tale begins with the "staples of the sentimental genre, particularly the qualities of purity and its opposite," but within "this familiar territory Hawthorne works with decidedly anti-sentimental themes."[7]

Theme appears largely a means for the male narrator to discover the material that will give him narratorial power over women. "Their bright eyes were fixed on me; their lips apart," he observes near the end of his narrative. "I took courage, and led the fated pair to a new-made grave, where for a few moments, in the bright and silent midnight, they stood alone" (11: 275). Since Hawthorne actually situates his narrator and readers within the tale's fictional world, he can represent every author's fantasy of controlling his readers' responses so completely that he feels as if he were leading them by the hand.

Ironically, however, the male narrator only partially succeeds in capturing and controlling his female listeners' attention. Narrating the tale of Leonard and Alice Doane and Walter Brome does cause the young women to fall into his power – to fix their eyes on him, part their lips, and allow him to lead them to the new-made grave. But they laugh when he finishes his narrative, suggesting that they haven't been seduced by the story at all. If the story ended at this point, it would leave us with the impression that women are resistant to the seductive power of male narratives. The tale, however, does not end with the ladies' laughter – or with them in control of the narrator–auditor relationship. Their laughter provokes the narrator to try another tack. Instead of a melodramatic story, he will resort to history. Taking advantage of their location – Gallows Hill – he conjures up the moment of the witches' executions, describing the witches one by one as they walk up Gallows Hill to be hanged. He describes the scaffold and the executions themselves. "But here my companions seized an arm on each side," he notes triumphantly; "their nerves were trembling; and sweeter victory still, I had reached the seldom trodden places of their hearts, and found the wellspring of their tears" (11: 279–80). Here again, content seems subordinate to effect, as the narrator seeks the formula that will evoke the most intense reader response.

As many scholars have noted, Hawthorne illustrates a distinction between truth and fiction in the two tales his narrator tells, and he gives the nod to truth-telling, or history, when it comes to affecting readers. The invented gothic tale of incest and murder is less compelling than the narration of "real" historical events. But this theoretical distinction tells only half the story, for Hawthorne still emphasizes the question of what will move ladies to tears. Arguably sexual in its sense of penetration, the narrator's "victory" fulfills a desire for power over women and women's emotions through the medium of storytelling. Mary Ventura even accuses the narrator of being a "sexual provocateur" and "rapist." The young women cry at the end of the story, she argues, "because they are tired, hungry, and frightened. And because they have been violated."[8] To the extent that Hawthorne was testing the author–audience relation, he seeks ways to penetrate young women's hearts and release a flood of emotion and tears.

"Roger Malvin's Burial"

None of Hawthorne's early tales fulfills the affective goal he marked out in "Alice Doane's Appeal" better than "Roger Malvin's Burial," for the tale shows Hawthorne ambushing the domestic project of women's fiction and toying with women's maternal sympathies. "Roger Malvin's Burial" is a brilliant tale of moral quandaries – one of Hawthorne's best examinations of ethical complexities, as Colacurcio brilliantly demonstrates, rooted in the recognition that we cannot be sure of our own motives.[9] As the wounded Reuben Bourne and Roger Malvin try to make their way out of the forest, they face a dilemma.

Malvin will not survive the long journey, and if Reuben waits with him, he will also perish. Malvin encourages him to leave, but Reuben insists on staying, even though he expects Malvin to die. Initially, calculated realism gives way to a sentimental need to bear witness at the death scene of a loved one. Complicating Reuben's situation, Roger Malvin has been "like a father" (10: 340) and is in fact the father of Reuben's fiancée (Dorcas). Hawthorne does a masterful job of making Reuben's decision as complicated as possible. Creating situations of moral complexity in which conventional standards of right and wrong provide little guidance represents one of Hawthorne's strengths as a storyteller.

In this case, Hawthorne even has Roger Malvin urge Reuben to go by appealing to his feelings for Dorcas and telling him what to tell her so as to place his behavior in the best light. That is, despite Reuben's fervid wish to remain, Malvin effectively makes him leave – sending his blessing for a happy marriage along with him (10: 344). The one condition Malvin imposes is that Reuben return to give him a decent burial. Reuben does leave, but Hawthorne casts many doubts on his motives – not suggesting that he has decided wrongly so much as noting that Reuben will never be sure of his reasons and, in fact, will be wracked with guilt at the suspicion that he has left for selfish reasons. In effect, there is no way for Reuben to get himself off the horns of the dilemma he has faced.

Thus, at the crucial moment in the story, when Dorcas asks of her father's fate, Reuben "felt it impossible to acknowledge, that his selfish love of life had hurried him away, before her father's fate was decided," and he allows her to believe that he witnessed Malvin's death and placed a tombstone over his grave (10: 348). Reuben never recovers from this lie of omission. His life deteriorates until finally, acting more from unconscious impulse than design, he returns to the very spot where Malvin died and shoots his own son, Cyrus, after mistaking him for a deer. Frederick Crews notes the "logic of compulsion" that governs the tale, and he argues that Reuben shoots Cyrus because, secretly, he believes he has murdered Roger Malvin. "It is a sacrificial murder dictated by Reuben's unconscious charge of patricide and by his inability to bring the charge directly against himself."[10] Crews tends to ignore Dorcas's role in the story, especially in this scene, but, intriguingly, Hawthorne shifts his narrative perspective to her at the very moment that Reuben fires the shot that kills their son:

> Perceiving the motion of some object behind a thick veil of undergrowth, he fired, with the instinct of a hunter and the aim of a practiced marksman. A low moan, which told his success, and by which even animals can express their dying agony, was unheeded by Reuben Bourne. What were the recollections now breaking upon him? (10: 356)

Hawthorne postpones discovery of Cyrus's body for two lengthy paragraphs not only to create and maintain readers' suspense. The content of the two paragraphs suggests other motives. In the first, he presents Reuben's recognition that he has found his way to the spot where he had left Roger Malvin eighteen years before. In the second, he switches point of view to focus on Dorcas as she makes preparations for supper. Little do she and the first-time reader realize that the spectacle they will soon have to consume is her son's dead body.

Even though we witness Reuben's gunshot and wonder what he has hit, by moving the narrative backward in time coincident with the shift to Dorcas's viewpoint, Hawthorne opens ironic distance between his readers and his female character. This distance widens upon a second reading because we know that Cyrus is dead by his father's hand all the while Dorcas prepares a supper he will never eat. But even on a first reading we suspect the worst. The shift to Dorcas raises our suspicions, just as such a shift does today in a horror movie. We know something awful is going to happen – in part, because Dorcas, an innocent woman, has been so blissfully preoccupied with domestic business. We can almost hear the suspenseful music in the background, building to a climax.

By bringing Dorcas center stage, Hawthorne brings the story forward to his female readers. In a lengthy paragraph describing her "preparations for their evening repast," he writes an apostrophe to domestic ideals – a veritable fairy tale of domesticity transported to the heart of the wilderness. The "snow-white cloth" and "bright pewter vessels" make this "one little spot of homely comfort, in the desolate heart of Nature." Dorcas even sings while she works. Her "voice danced through the gloomy forest" (10: 357), while Hawthorne emphasizes that "four continually-recurring lines shone out from the rest, like the blaze of the hearth whose joys they celebrated. Into them, working magic with a few simple words, the poet had instilled the very essence of domestic love and household happiness, and they were poetry and picture joined in one" (10: 358).

This excerpt from a lengthy passage illustrates the rhetorical lengths to which Hawthorne went to evoke a spirit of domestic security and harmony. But this paragraph occupies a space between the moment when Reuben fires his gun and Dorcas hears the shot. Hawthorne follows the passage I quoted with the following sentence: "She was aroused by the report of a gun, in the vicinity of the encampment; and either the sudden sound, or her loneliness by the glowing fire, caused her to tremble violently. The next moment, she laughed in the pride of a mother's heart." "My beautiful young hunter!" she exclaims; "my boy has slain a deer!" (10: 358).

With that ironic line, Hawthorne keeps up the suspense and feeds the hope that Cyrus really has killed a deer, despite the violent trembling that the shot evokes in Dorcas. Hawthorne plays with Dorcas's emotions by allowing her to feel pride in Cyrus even as he lies dead on the ground just out of view. The emotional "high" of her mother's pride sets Dorcas (and the female reader) up for an even greater emotional "fall." Hawthorne then follows Dorcas into the woods and, from her point of view, finally shows the expectant reader the result of Reuben's shot:

> Oh! there lay the boy, asleep, but dreamless, upon the fallen
> forest-leaves! his cheek rested upon his arm, his curled locks were
> thrown back from his brow, his limbs were slightly relaxed. Had a
> sudden weariness overcome the youthful hunter? Would his mother's
> voice arouse him? She knew that it was death.   (10: 360)

Even at this moment, Hawthorne mocks sentimental tropes of death as sleep – raising the brief hope that Cyrus only sleeps before confirming his death and mocking, with his rhetorical question, the impotence of the "mother's voice." Dorcas's subjectivity can express itself only in a "wild shriek" (10: 360). It has no other power. In interrupting his frontier narrative with the gunshot and extended domestic scene, Hawthorne might seem to be making a concession to female readers. Dorcas's scene, however, is little more than a commercial interruption. Hawthorne's intuition – creating suspense with a gunshot and then filling the interval with a cozy scene of homemaking – at once advertises his sentimental powers and turns them against the readers whose attention he has captured. Dorcas's homemaking enables more than it interrupts Hawthorne's frontier plot-making. She leaves her frontier hearth and home ready for a homecoming she will never enjoy.

"The Gentle Boy"

We can better understand Hawthorne's strategies and the relationship he establishes with female readers in "Roger Malvin's Burial" by examining "The Gentle Boy," a tale that he revised for the 1837 *Twice-Told Tales* and also published by itself in January 1839 as a "Thrice Told Tale" – with "An Original Illustration" by Sophia advertised on the title page. Like "Roger Malvin's Burial," "The Gentle Boy" features bad or careless parenting that leads to a child's death, but Hawthorne's treatments of the death scenes differ dramatically.

While Ilbrahim's Quaker mother (Catharine) exemplifies the careless parenting Hawthorne had described in such tales as "The Hollow of the Three Hills," Tobias and Dorothy Pearson represent a more positive model when they take Ilbrahim into their home after his father is executed and his mother disappears. Treated gently by his new parents, Ilbrahim flourishes, becoming a "domesticated sunbeam" (9: 89), but his rehabilitation as a gentle boy has unfortunate consequences. When he befriends a boy who was injured near the Pearson home and then attempts to play with other Puritan children, "all at once the devil of their fathers entered into the unbreeched fanatics," who, like "a brood of baby-fiends," beat him with sticks and stones with "an instinct of destruction, far more loathsome than the blood-thirstiness of manhood." The very boy Ilbrahim befriended leads the charge and strikes Ilbrahim on the mouth "so forcibly that the blood issued in a stream" (9: 92).

If the attack on Ilbrahim is bloodier and more violent than Cyrus Bourne's death off stage in "Roger Malvin's Burial," Hawthorne's treatment of the two deaths illustrates the different relationships he established with his audience. "The Gentle Boy" features straightforward sentimentality, as Ilbrahim lies on his deathbed and brings characters and readers alike into his emotional orbit. Indeed, Hawthorne doubles the pleasure this deathbed scene affords by bringing not one, but two mothers into the room. First he focuses on Dorothy Pearson's feelings, as the dying Ilbrahim takes her hand. She "almost imagined that she could discern the near, though dim delightfulness, of the home he was about to reach; she would not have enticed the little wanderer back, though she bemoaned herself that she must leave him and return" (9: 103). Heaven as superior to earth, a martyr's death superior to life in a demonic Puritan stronghold – these are terms designed to bring author, characters, and readers into a state of emotional communion. Then, when Catharine enters the room, "she drew Ilbrahim to her bosom, and he nestled there, with no violence of joy, but contentedly as if he were hushing himself to sleep. He looked into her face, and reading its agony, said, with feeble earnestness, 'Mourn not, dearest mother. I am happy now.' And with these words, the gentle boy was dead" (9: 103–04). Restoring the estranged Catharine to her role as his "dear mother," Ilbrahim heals and blesses fractured family relationships. The happiness of his death contrasts with the horrible catharsis that attends Cyrus Bourne's – catharsis for his father, if not for his mother, whose "wild shriek" registers emotional violence far exceeding the quiet "agony" that Ilbrahim assuages.

Although Hawthorne originally published "The Gentle Boy" and "Roger Malvin's Burial" in the same year (1832), he included "The Gentle Boy" in the 1837 edition of *Twice-Told Tales* but waited until 1846 to republish "Roger Malvin's Burial" in *Mosses from an Old Manse*. Hawthorne also held "Young Goodman Brown" out of *Twice-Told Tales*, even though he had published the story in 1835.

"Young Goodman Brown"

"Young Goodman Brown," one of Hawthorne's most complex tales, explores the frustrating fact that we can never know the contents of another person's mind. Many critics consider this tale Hawthorne's best effort to come to terms with the Salem witch trials in 1692, and the tale depends heavily on the credibility of the sort of "specter evidence" that played such an important role in the conviction of the Salem witches.[11] But at its center, when Goodman Brown turns to his wife Faith with the injunction, "Look up to Heaven and resist the wicked one," the story reduces to this question of inscrutability: Brown can never know for sure whether Faith, or any other of the assembled townspeople, has actually resisted temptation.

In this respect, Goodman Brown's ethical situation resembles Reuben Bourne's; he must wrestle with his ability to know other people's motives and his own. In both cases Hawthorne suggests that such knowledge is elusive and probably impossible to obtain. He also demonstrates the cost for such characters of not being able to accept the reality of an ambiguous, gray (rather than black and white) world both inside and outside the individual self. Goodman Brown concludes, for example, that everyone has given in to Satan's temptations – that he is the only "good man" left in town – and he distrusts his neighbors and his wife for the rest of his gloomy life. Hawthorne thereby critiques Puritan introspectiveness – the tendency to examine oneself for evidence of salvation – but the ideas that Goodman Brown's situation illustrates certainly transcend that historical time and place. For one thing, Hawthorne toys with his readers throughout the tale, suggesting that Goodman Brown is only dreaming. In this respect the story exemplifies Hawthorne's sometimes frustrating tendency to give evidence with one hand and take it back with the other – to create ambiguity of human perception and conclusion, leaving us suspended in a subjective, indeterminate realm with no stable ground.

Hawthorne uses the forest in "Young Goodman Brown" traditionally – as space liberated from custom and homely values, an underground where dark impulses rise from the unconscious. From one point of view Brown has his own special type of midsummer night's dream – a nightmare formed out of Puritan materials. As he journeys into the forest, he becomes less and less sure of objective reality. The solid ground gives way beneath his feet, as he enters a world of dark fantasy – his own dark fantasies and speculations about others. The first man he meets looks like his own father; the staff the man carries looks like a "great black snake, so curiously wrought that it might almost be seen to twist and wriggle itself like a living serpent" – but this may be only an "ocular deception" (10: 76). Brown meets Goody Cloyse, the woman who taught him his catechism – she too apparently headed for a meeting with the Devil. He hears voices that he identifies as those of the minister and Deacon Gookin. He even catches a pink ribbon that flutters onto a branch and recognizes – or thinks he recognizes – the very ribbon that his new wife Faith was wearing in her hair when he left her that afternoon. Goodman Brown is on a dangerous mission – just how dangerous becomes clear when he finally finds himself among the "grave and dark-clad company" (10: 84) assembled for a Black Mass in "the heart of the dark wilderness" (10: 83).

There follows one of the most remarkable passages Hawthorne ever wrote – a vision of social and domestic evil that would shake anyone's faith in the integrity of others. As Satan turns to Goodman Brown, as if to introduce him to the company, whom he "has reverenced from youth," he promises:

> This night it shall be granted you to know their secret deeds; how hoary-bearded elders of the church have whispered wanton words to the young maids of their households; how many a woman, eager for widow's weeds, has given her husband a drink at bed-time and let him sleep his last sleep in her bosom; how beardless youths have made haste to inherit their fathers' wealth; and how fair damsels – blush not, sweet ones! – have dug little graves in the garden, and bidden me, the sole guest, to an infant's funeral.　(10: 87)

Hawthorne was a master psychologist, as well as well-read historian, and the vision of evil to which he treats Goodman Brown has its origins inside as much as outside the character. As Satan explains, "By the sympathy of your human hearts for sin, ye shall scent out all the places – whether in church, bed-chamber, street, field, or forest – where crime has been committed, and shall exult to behold the whole earth one stain of guilt, one mighty blood-spot" (10: 87). The key word is "sympathy," which means sympathetic identification – the capacity to recognize impulses in oneself that one sees in others. The Puritans, at least as Hawthorne depicts them, prefer to brand and scapegoat others and to ostracize them from the community – in effect, denying and purging the sinfulness in their own characters. During the Salem witchcraft hysteria in 1692, the good people of Salem hanged nineteen alleged witches and pressed another to death.

Ironically, in "Young Goodman Brown," Brown out-Puritans the Puritans, concluding that he remains the only good man in a society of sinners. He may, as Hawthorne suggests, have "fallen asleep in the forest, and only dreamed a wild dream of a witch-meeting" (10: 89), but the effect is the same. Even though he lives a superficially ordinary life – complete with children and grandchildren – he estranges himself morally and emotionally from others. "A stern, a sad, a darkly meditative, a distrustful, if not a desperate man, did he become, from the night of that fearful dream" (10: 89), and when they bear him to his grave, "they carved no hopeful verse upon his tomb-stone; for his dying hour was gloom" (10: 90). Given its dark themes and the horrific vision of domestic plotting and violence it includes, it is not surprising that Hawthorne chose not to include "Young Goodman Brown" in his first collection of tales.

"The May-Pole of Merry Mount"

Hawthorne did include "The May-Pole of Merry Mount" in the 1837 edition of *Twice-Told Tales* and another, related tale of the Puritans, "Endicott and the Red Cross," in the expanded edition of *Twice-Told Tales* he published in 1842. Although neither tale features the psychological and moral complexity we find in "Young Goodman Brown" or other better-known tales, each of them helps us understand Hawthorne's complex attitude toward Puritanism and also shows him trying out ideas that he would develop in *The Scarlet Letter*.

Edgar and Edith, the young betrothed couple in "The May-Pole of Merry Mount," face some of the same challenges as Hester Prynne and Arthur Dimmesdale, as they find themselves trying to act on their passionate feelings in the face of stern Puritan authority. "Jollity and gloom were contending for an empire," Hawthorne announces in the tale's first paragraph (9: 54), and those contending values focus on the young couple. Based on the settlement at Mount Wollaston that Thomas Morton established in 1627 in opposition to the Plymouth Colony, Merry Mount posed a threat to Puritan hegemony and was eventually burned to the ground by order of Massachusetts Bay Governor John Winthrop. Hawthorne's story is based on an earlier event, when John Endicott invaded the settlement and cut down the maypole that Morton had erected. Set on midsummer's eve, the narrative shows the maypole decked out gaudily for worship by a "wild throng" of Fauns and Nymphs who resemble "Gothic monsters" (9: 55). Hawthorne loved to write crowd scenes, most of them featuring carnivalesque revelry and character disguise and suggesting a relaxation of conventional rules of human identity and behavior. The Black Mass in "Young Goodman Brown" is a good example. In "The May-Pole of Merry Mount" he makes the crowd of nature-worshippers the focal point of his story, and he seems to sympathize with the designs of this "gay colony" to "pour sunshine over New England's rugged hills, and scatter flower-seeds throughout the soil" (9: 54). Ominously, he also describes a "band of Puritans, who watched the scene," and "compared the masques to those devils and ruined souls, with whom their superstition peopled the black wilderness" (90). Posing one utopian colony against another, Hawthorne anticipates the rebellion against Calvinist authority that would evolve into the Unitarian and Transcendentalist movements of the nineteenth century, emphasizing self-reliance, the importance of inner light and intuition, the influence of nature and natural impulses, and the power of individuals to "consecrate" their own acts according to higher laws.

Although Hawthorne seems to make the battle between the Puritans and the Merry Mounters an even one, the historical record operates like fate on the facts of the story. "The future complexion of New England was involved in this important quarrel," he announces.

> Should the grisly saints establish their jurisdiction over the gay sinners, then would their spirits darken all the clime, and make it a land of clouded visages, of hard toil, of sermon and psalm, forever. But should the banner-staff of Merry Mount be fortunate, sunshine would break upon the hills, and flowers would beautify the forest, and late posterity do homage to the May-Pole! (9: 62)

John Endicott, the "Puritan of Puritans" (9: 63), cuts down the maypole and orders whippings for the revelers. As Hawthorne wryly observes, the whipping post "might be termed the Puritan May-Pole" (9: 61). If there is any suspense, it resides in the fate of Edgar and Edith. While one of the Puritans advises a "double share of stripes" for the couple, even the "iron man," Endicott, is "softened" (9: 66) by the picture of their "youthful beauty," which, "in the first hour of wedlock," seemed "so pure and high" (9: 65). Instead of physical punishment, Edgar and Edith will be re-educated. They are dressed immediately in "garments of a more decent fashion," while Edgar's hair is "cropt" in the "true pumpkin-shell fashion" (9: 66). The story ends quickly with a flash forward to the very end of the couple's lives and the observation that they "went heavenward, supporting each other along the difficult path which it was their lot to tread and never wasted one regretful thought on the vanities of Merry Mount" (9: 67). Edgar and Edith never find the strength to declare that Merry Mount has a "consecration of its own," but Hawthorne's careful language at the end of the tale suggests that the maypole-worshipping settlement might have presented them with a less "difficult" path than their conscription into the Puritan community – even if they don't waste their thoughts on that alternative.

"Endicott and the Red Cross"

"Endicott and the Red Cross" (1838) is a slighter tale, but it features the same John Endicott in the same intolerant, punitive role. In this case, however, Endicott also gets to be the hero of the story, as he declares the colony's independence from British rule. Hawthorne thus depicts two extremes of Puritanism. Anticipating the pan shot of modern movie-making, he scans the street of Salem village, noting the "grim" and still bloody head of a wolf, "nailed on the porch of the meetinghouse," the whipping post, pillory, and stocks. He notes a man and woman standing side-by-side on the meetinghouse steps – he bearing the label, A WANTON GOSPELLER, on his breast (9: 434), she wearing a cleft stick on her tongue, "in appropriate retribution for having wagged that unruly member against the elders of the church" (9: 435). He notes that

> among the crowd were several, whose punishment would be life-long; some, whose ears had been cropt, like those of puppy-dogs; others, whose cheeks had been branded with the initials of their misdemeanors; one, with his nostrils slit and seared; and another, with a halter about his neck. (9: 435)

Most important for the sake of artistic posterity, Hawthorne lingers on a

> young woman, with no mean share of beauty, whose doom it was to wear the letter A on the breast of her gown, in the eyes of all the world and her own children. And even her own children knew what that initial signified. Sporting with her infamy, the lost and desperate creature had embroidered the fatal token in scarlet cloth, with golden thread and the nicest art of needle-work; so that the capital A might have been thought to mean Admirable, or anything rather than Adultress. (9: 435)

Remarkably, many seeds from this passage germinate and sprout in *The Scarlet Letter* – the woman's beauty, the letter itself, its embroidery in gold thread, its subtle change in meaning at the woman's hand, the negotiation of meaning between the woman and the people observing her. In this long list of Puritan punishments, Hawthorne illustrates the dark hegemony they wielded over dissent and dissenters.

It is the more ironic, then, that John Endicott should speak up so loudly and compellingly for freedom. "Wherefore," Endicott intones, "have we sought this country of a rugged soil and wintry sky? Was it not for the enjoyment of our civil rights? Was it not for liberty to worship God according to our conscience?" (9: 439). No wonder the Wanton Gospeller interrupts with the question, "Call you this liberty of conscience?" (9: 439). Nevertheless, Endicott continues with a declaration of independence from British intrusion and British rule, and he climaxes his speech by cutting the red cross out of the British flag (9: 440). "With a cry of triumph, the people gave their sanction to one of the boldest exploits which our history records," Hawthorne concludes. "We look back through the mist of ages, and recognize, in the rending of the Red Cross from New England's banner, the first omen of that deliverance which our fathers consummated, after the bones of the stern Puritan had lain more than a century in the dust" (9: 441). Hawthorne refers to the Revolutionary War, and his praise suggests continuity rather than opposition between that war and the Puritans' early efforts to establish a foothold in America. He certainly makes John Endicott a hard person to admire – history is often made by despicable individuals – but he struck a blow for religious freedom that would help solidify the foundation on which the Colonies could declare themselves independent of British authority.

Many of Hawthorne's stories had their origins in brief observations he copied into his notebooks. "A snake, taken into a man's stomach and nourished there from fifteen years to thirty-five, tormenting him most horribly" – this 1836 entry develops into "Egotism; or, The Bosom Serpent" (first published in the *Democratic Review* in 1843).[12] "A man to flatter himself with the idea that he would be guilty of some certain wickedness, – as, for instance, to yield to the personal temptations of the Devil" (8: 25) – this entry provides the germ for "Young Goodman Brown." And most famously, in an 1845 entry Hawthorne wrote: "The life of a woman, who, by the old colony law, was condemned to wear the letter A, sewed on her garment, in token of her having committed adultery" (8: 254). Hawthorne had already included such a woman in "Endicott and the Red Cross," but the key addition in the notebook is the word "life." Four years before he sat down to write *The Scarlet Letter*, he could imagine writing a narrative about the "life of a woman" who wears a scarlet letter.

"The Minister's Black Veil"

Hawthorne had an uncanny ability to spot the potential significance of such germs. Many of his best tales depend upon an existential premise – a premise whose elaboration uncovers some fundamental truth about the inner life, or identity, of an individual or an individual's most basic relationship to other people or the physical world. Like Franz Kafka's "The Metamorphosis," "The Minister's Black Veil" explores the idea of what happens when a man drastically changes his appearance. Does he become someone else, or does some fundamental core of identity remain, transcending changes in outward appearance and personal circumstance? Hawthorne does a brilliant job of examining the range of public responses to this extraordinary action, as well as their effect on the minister. He never reveals the motive behind Reverend Hooper's decision to wear a veil. He cares more about exploring the social effect of that decision. What happens to our relationship with others – to the identity we have for others – and even for ourselves – when we make such a drastic, even if superficial, change in ourselves? When he places a black veil over his face, the Reverend Hooper not only estranges himself from his parishioners, but he fundamentally alters his own perception of himself.

The black veil thus anticipates the scarlet letter. Though self-imposed rather than imposed from without, the veil marks its wearer and offers, in place of the whole person, a sign of selfhood that people must read and interpret. The townspeople assume that Mr. Hooper wears the veil for a particular reason, and readers face the same challenge of trying to see behind the veil to the minister's motives. Edgar Allan Poe thought he had solved the mystery. When the Reverend Hooper attends the funeral of a young lady and stoops beside the corpse, a "superstitious old woman" reports that the "corpse had slightly shuddered" (9: 42). With some self-satisfaction, Poe commented: "that a crime of dark dye, (having reference to the 'young lady') has been committed, is a point which only minds congenial with that of the author will perceive."[13] This tale, like others, however, renders motives and the individual self ambiguous, opaque rather than transparent – that is, veiled. Even when Elizabeth, his fiancée, asks him to remove the veil for her, he refuses. "This dismal shade must separate me from the world," he tells her, "even you, Elizabeth, can never come behind it" (9: 46). In effect, Mr. Hooper asks Elizabeth to accept him on faith – ultimately, we recognize, a necessity in any human relationship. However much we may want others to be transparent, however much we believe that they are transparent, "The Minister's Black Veil" suggests that we are fooling ourselves. As Mr. Hooper says, "I look around me, and, lo! On every visage a Black Veil!" (9: 52).

Readers are in the same frustrating position as Mr. Hooper's parishioners. In J. Hillis Miller's terms, "the story is an allegory of the reader's own situation in reading it."[14] The townspeople's relationship to the veil resembles our relationship to "The Minister's Black Veil" – the story of that name, as well as the piece of black crape. Hawthorne after all is the one who decided to place the veil on Hooper's face and then to tantalize us with possible explanations for why it's there. Is it a sign of some secret sin or crime (as Poe thought)? Is it a more generalized symbol of human depravity and sinfulness? Is it a mask that protects Mr. Hooper from others, or others from him? Is it a lens through which he sees the world darkly? Is it a screen on which others can project their fantasies? Is it even perhaps an early example of blackface, a reference to color-coding and race and the arbitrariness of those signifiers of human identity? (John F. Birk argues that "The Minister's Black Veil" bears traces of the slavery issue and sees William Lloyd Garrison behind Hooper's veil.)[15] Ironically, wearing the black veil improves Hooper's preaching performance: "there was something, either in the sentiment of the discourse itself, or in the imagination of the auditors, which made [his sermon] the most powerful effort that they had ever heard from their pastor's lips" (9: 40).

In this tale and in others Hawthorne tests the proposition that human identity is contingent and circumstantial, rather than an inherent essence – that is, not an identity at all. We like to think that there is something in us – a soul, or some other core of identity, the continuity that memory gives us – that does not change. We may change, but at some deep level we remain the same person. Indeed, it is hard to think of ourselves in any other way; for if we do not have such a core essence in us, how do we know ourselves at all? This is precisely the problem that Reverend Hooper faces. Not only does he become a monster to his parishioners; he becomes a monster to himself. Putting on the veil eventually causes him not to recognize himself. Catching a "glimpse of his figure in the looking-glass, the black veil involved his own spirit in the horror with which it overwhelmed all others" (9: 43–44). Parson Hooper's wearing of the veil, in J. Hillis Miller's view, "suspends two of the assumptions that make society possible: the assumption that a person's face is the sign of his selfhood and the accompanying presumption that this sign can in one way or another be read" (*Hawthorne and History*, 92).

"Wakefield"

"Wakefield" elaborates a similar idea in the form of a common fantasy – to die or disappear but retain the power to see what effect your absence has on the people and the world you left behind. Washington Irving's "Rip Van Winkle" (1821) explores this idea, as Rip sleeps through the Revolutionary War before returning to the town that he left twenty years before. In Hawthorne's tale, Wakefield leaves his wife and home one day, apparently on a whim, and he settles nearby so that he can watch his wife react to his absence. In effect, Wakefield steps outside of time, becoming "another man" – an invisible man – and leaving an absence where his presence used to be (9: 135). As Sharon Cameron puts it, "He wants feeling to be outside of him, to be felt for rather than by him."[16] In Hawthorne's terms,

> It was Wakefield's unprecedented fate, to retain his original share of human sympathies, and to be still involved in human interests, while he had lost his reciprocal influence on them. It would be a most curious speculation, to trace out the effect of such circumstances on his heart and intellect, separately, and in unison. Yet, changed as he was, he would seldom be conscious of it, but deem himself the same man as before.
>
> (9: 138)

Wakefield, like Rip Van Winkle, also flees a particular situation – his wife and the domestic sphere of marriage and home he associates with her. In this respect the story enacts an exaggerated version of the common nineteenth-century paradigm of separate spheres. Mrs. Wakefield remains within the home, while Wakefield makes another life for himself outside it. Not that Wakefield's flight is motivated by such considerations. Hawthorne never explains the reasons for Wakefield's escape, any more than he tells us why Reverend Hooper dons the black veil. He even suggests that Wakefield himself does not know his motives. And at the end of the tale, when Wakefield decides to return home, his decision seems a product of whim, the result of pausing one night before his house and noticing the "comfortable fire" on the hearth. As he does in "The Minister's Black Veil," Hawthorne draws a curtain of ambiguity over the question of human motivation.

"My Kinsman, Major Molineux"

"My Kinsman, Major Molineux" also explores the foundations of identity. A classic coming-of-age story in which the young Robin Molineux leaves his country home for the city of Boston, where he hopes to trade upon his kinsman's name and position and so make his way in the world, the tale presents Robin in traditional fashion as "a youth of barely eighteen years, evidently country-bred, and now, as it would seem, upon his first visit to town."[17] Already we have a pretty good idea of what will follow. Robin will have his values tested. He will become lost in the city. He will lose himself in some sense. There will probably be a woman involved. He may gain a new self – perhaps an older and wiser one. Hawthorne's primary variation on this old story resides in the particular situation he describes – the political turmoil involving Robin's kinsman, Major Molineux – but the tale represents another of his early efforts to test the terms and limits of individual identity.

Although he carries an oak cudgel, suggesting support by the natural country life he has led, Robin identifies himself immediately with his city-based kinsman. (Hawthorne opens the tale by identifying Major Molineux, the colonial governor appointed by the king, with a half dozen governors against whom the American colonists rebelled.) Each time he asks directions, he identifies Major Molineux as his uncle, not realizing, of course, that the people he asks are plotting his uncle's overthrow that very evening. Spurned by a stranger, Robin resorts to class distinctions, convinced that the man is not good enough to have "seen the inside of my kinsman's door" (11: 211). When an innkeeper treats him respectfully, Robin attributes the respect to the man's recognition of the "family likeness": "the rogue has guessed that I am related to the Major!"

(11: 213). However, when Robin condescendingly identifies himself as Major Molineux's kinsman, the innkeeper points to a paper on the wall – a wanted poster for a runaway indentured servant – and suggests that Robin himself is the fugitive (11: 214). Clearly, identity remains fluid in this story. If Robin attempts to identify himself using external indicators – his connection to Major Molineux – he opens up the possibility that others will identify him using different markers.

Sexual initiation nearly always accompanies such country-to-city journeys, and Hawthorne flirts with that possibility in Robin's case, when he asks after his kinsman at the house of a woman wearing a scarlet petticoat: "She was a dainty little figure, with a white neck, round arms, and a slender waist, at the extremity of which her scarlet petticoat jutted out over a hoop . . . and her bright eyes possessed a sly freedom, which triumphed over those of Robin" (11: 217). From Robin's point of view, this description suggests the once-over of the male gaze, surveying a woman's body, but in this case Robin's male gaze meets its match, as the young woman stares him down. Furthermore, she slyly tells him that the Major dwells in the house – indeed, has been "a-bed this hour or more" (11: 217). Inviting Robin to cross the threshold in his uncle's name, she takes him by the hand and proceeds to drag "his half-willing footsteps" almost into the house, before a noise in the neighborhood causes her to vanish (11: 218). Robin clearly does not know his uncle, and it is only at the end of the story that we as readers understand that Major Molineux cannot help Robin rise in the world. But this scene of attempted seduction tells us that the Major may be living a life quite different from what the innocent Robin imagines and may not be the person on whom to pin his hopes.

As he does in "Young Goodman Brown," Hawthorne opens the possibility that Robin's experience is a dream, and from this point on, like Goodman Brown, Robin grows increasingly disoriented. "He now roamed desperately, and at random, through the town, almost ready to believe that spell was on him" (11: 219), and this accelerating journey results in his arrival, like Brown, at a vantage point from which he can watch the evening's staged events. The extended vision that concludes the tale immerses Robin in the realm of romance. Indeed, Hawthorne notes that the moon, "'creating, like the imaginative power, a beautiful strangeness in familiar objects,' gave something of romance to a scene, that might not have possessed it in the light of day" (11: 221). Hawthorne is experimenting – and calling attention to his experimentation – with special effects, his power to create an imaginary world, or neutral territory, in which dream and reality dissolve into one another. Robin, Goodman Brown, and other characters in Hawthorne's early fiction play the role of readers or interpreters within the work. Their visions and experiences originate from within themselves. That is, Hawthorne tests his ability to penetrate a reader's mind with a story that registers unconsciously, but powerfully, and thereby captures the reader's attention almost against his (or her) will because the content already exists there in the form of unconscious fears and desires. Frederick Crews asks "whether Robin's own mind may not be the chief referent of Hawthorne's symbols," and he emphasizes the Oedipal fantasies of dependence on and resentment of paternal figures of authority that culminate in Robin's joining the colonists in a ritual of degrading the Major.[18] The phantasmagoric experiences that climax the tale and result in Robin's shouting even louder than the rest of the townspeople at his uncle's "humiliation" and "foul disgrace" (11: 229), after all, resemble a "dream" that has "broken forth from some feverish brain" and is "sweeping visibly through the midnight streets" (11: 228). Hawthorne suggests that more than Robin's personal desires are in play – that such revolutionary moments originate in a collective fantasy or dream (rebellion against paternal authority) with which Robin identifies.

T. Walter Herbert has pointed out that "My Kinsman, Major Molineux" "portrays the quandary of a young man who carries the social habits of deferential hierarchy into the era of their revolutionary overthrow." Robin himself undergoes a "psychological revolution," in Herbert's view, repudiating his uncle and being initiated "into the world of self-made men."[19] The end of the story is not quite so clear, however, for we cannot tell whether Robin intends to stay in the city or return home, or whether he has learned the lesson that the benevolent stranger provides: "if you prefer to remain with us, perhaps, as you are a shrewd youth, you may rise in the world, without the help of your kinsman, Major Molineux" (11: 231).

"Monsieur du Miroir"

Hawthorne wrote in the midst of many social reform movements, and when we consider gender identities and constructs as a context in which to situate him and his writing, we must consider the male purity movement and especially some of the advice manuals for men published during the middle of the nineteenth century. Hawthorne's "Monsieur du Miroir" (1837) illustrates his concern for the issues raised by male reformers – issues involving male continence, integrity, and self-control. As manhood came under increasing pressures for self-making and success, imitative and other-directed concepts of male identity met head-on with romantic notions of self-reliant, even narcissistic male identity.

Nineteenth-century America represented the heyday of individualism, epitomized by Ralph Waldo Emerson's essay "Self Reliance" (1841). "To believe your own thought, to believe that what is true for you in your private heart, is true for all men," Emerson famously wrote, "that is genius."[20] Hawthorne might have longed for such confidence, but his fiction typically portrays such believers as obsessed and mad. David Leverenz notes that Hawthorne's "fascination with marketplace humiliation reflects a profound quarrel with the manhood he feels inside himself, so narcissistically needy for self-empowering through malice and cruelty."[21] Leverenz's Hawthorne – narcissistic, fearful, over-compensating – is not self-reliant, but co-dependent. A manly self-image depends upon other men's confirmation. In "Monsieur du Miroir" Hawthorne tests the limits and dangers of self-reliance, which proves risky in the form of self-mirroring. Self-reliance and self-making can become self-pollution.

Hawthorne must have been aware that the sketch would enter a shrill conversation about male purity. Sylvester Graham's widely popular *Lecture to Young Men on Chastity* had appeared only three years before, warning its readers against the dangers of "lascivious day-dreams" and "amorous reveries," which for men are "often the sources of general debility, effeminacy, disordered functions, and permanent disease."[22] Graham and others generalized their advice to include the dangers of reading fiction, and posited a slippery slope from reading to reverie to masturbation and from masturbation to a host of mental and bodily evils. The "secret and solitary vice" (44) threatens male subjectivity by disrupting proper object relations and the mirroring service they provide. Masturbators "cannot meet the look of others," Graham claims, especially the looks of women (45). Manhood, Graham suggests, must not only be mirrored but mirrored by women – that is, constructed through a female gaze. The alternative is a gothic horror of narcissism that leads down a slippery slope to homosexuality, as Graham suggests that a fixation on one's own self can lead to a love of other men. "I have known boys," Graham insists, "almost entirely ruined in health and constitution, by this destructive practice; and they have assured me, that, to their certain knowledge, almost every boy in the school practiced the filthy vice; and many of them went to the still more loathsome and criminal extent of an unnatural commerce with each other!" (43).

Hawthorne recognized the importance of emerging from narcissistic reveries and investing himself emotionally in someone else, but forming a productive object-relation proves difficult in the sketch. "Once, presumptuous that he was," Monsieur du Miroir "even stole into the heaven of a young lady's eyes, so that while I gazed, and was dreaming only of herself, I found him also in my dream" (9: 165). Hawthorne wishes in vain that M. du Miroir could be persuaded to transfer his attachment to someone else, leaving him (the narrator) to form a pure relation with a young lady. "If I must needs have so intrusive an intimate, who stares me in the face in my closest privacy, and follows me even to my bed-chamber, I should prefer – scandal apart – the laughing bloom of a young girl, to the dark and bearded gravity of my present companion" (9: 166). On the verge of being trapped in the auto/homo-erotic closet, Hawthorne looks longingly toward a transgressive heterosexuality, to a blooming young girl in his bedroom to save him from himself and from this "other" desire. Arthur Dimmesdale and Miles Coverdale face the same problem and solve it momentarily in the same way before retreating to their bachelors' quarters and their studies. Hawthorne himself, in contrast, worked hard once he met Sophia Peabody in 1837 (the same year he published "Monsieur du Miroir") to renounce bachelorhood and bachelor quarters for a married life of what he projected to be marital bliss.

After Hawthorne married Sophia Peabody in 1842 and moved to the Old Manse in Concord, Massachusetts, he started writing a new collection of tales, *Mosses from an Old Manse* (1846). Hawthorne's private writings testify to his emotional and psychological dependence upon Sophia. He considered her his "second self" (16: 9), and in a letter to Longfellow (27 March 1845) he referred to himself as "extant in a threefold capacity; my wife and little girl making up the complete individual" (16: 84). Sophia provided all the companionship he thought he needed, and he ecstatically contrasted his life with her to his lonely bachelorhood. "My wife is, in the strictest sense, my sole companion," he wrote in his journal; "and I need no other – there is no vacancy in my mind, any more than in my heart" (8: 367). When they were separated in November 1844 – he in Salem, she in Boston with her family – he wrote, "there is a great vacuity caused by thy absence out of my daily life – a bottomless abyss, into which all minor contentments might be flung without filling it up" (16: 68). As these passages suggest, the newly married Hawthorne was defining himself relationally rather than narcissistically. He was discovering the advantages, as well as some of the anxieties, of interdependent selfhood – the satisfactions and anxieties of being a husband and a father.

Our current view of Hawthorne, especially the Hawthorne who explored the dark underside of human consciousness, owes a great deal to the lengthy review essay Herman Melville wrote about *Mosses from an Old Manse*. Melville's two-part essay, "Hawthorne and His Mosses," appeared shortly after their initial meeting (in 1850) and still represents one of the most insightful early analyses of Hawthorne's writing. Even though Melville's perception of a "blackness" in Hawthorne's fiction reveals as much about his own preoccupation as a writer as it does about Hawthorne's, he did highlight aspects of Hawthorne's writing that stand in sharp contrast, for example, to the "sweet" facets of his tales that Longfellow had praised earlier. The world is "mistaken" in Hawthorne, Melville would famously observe. "For spite of the Indian-summer sunlight on the hither side of Hawthorne's soul, the other side – like the dark half of the physical sphere – is shrouded in a blackness, ten times black."[23]

Even though he had originally written them a decade before, Hawthorne included the dark tales "Young Goodman Brown" and "Roger Malvin's Burial" in *Mosses from an Old Manse*. Several of the other stories in *Mosses from an Old Manse*, especially "The Birth-mark," "The Artist of the Beautiful," "Rappaccini's Daughter," and "Drowne's Wooden Image," mark out a new direction that leads to the long romances – the representation and intense engagement with issues in gender identity and roles, as well as with male–female relationships. Most of these stories also have their dark side, especially when read from a woman's point of view. Hawthorne's marriage gave him an intimate knowledge of women that he had been lacking and also challenged his imagination in ways that sponsored some of his strongest writing. The male protagonists in each of these tales illustrate issues that male artists face in creating female characters, especially when those characters have lives of their own.

Hawthorne had clearly been fascinated by powerful women who can stand up for themselves and intimidate men, as early works such as "Mrs. Hutchinson" (1830) and "The Gentle Boy" (1832) will demonstrate. Although "Mrs. Hutchinson" paints a somewhat negative portrait of its subject, Ann Hutchinson stands "loftily" before her male judges, whom "her doctrines have put in fear." The "deepest controversialists of that scholastic day," Hawthorne notes, "find here a woman, whom all their trained and sharpened intellects are inadequate to foil" (23: 72). Raining down accusations upon their heads, Hutchinson anticipates Catharine, the Quaker woman who usurps male prerogatives and the pulpit in "The Gentle Boy" in order to harangue the congregation, while the minister sits in "speechless and almost terrified astonishment" (9:80). Although he questions her motives, Hawthorne clearly admires her power, which he associates with his own power as a writer:

> it was a vague and incomprehensible rhapsody, which, however, seemed
> to spread its own atmosphere round the hearer's soul, and to move
> his feelings by some influence unconnected with the words. As she
> proceeded, beautiful but shadowy images would sometimes be seen, like
> bright things moving in a turbid river; or a strong and singularly shaped
> idea leapt forth, and seized at once on the understanding or the heart.
>
> (9:81)

"The New Adam and Eve"

The tales Hawthorne wrote after his marriage, during the three years that he and Sophia lived at the Old Manse in Concord, tell a more complicated story. Even though he wrote down the premise for "The New Adam and Eve" as early as 1836 (8: 21), it seems likely that his marriage inspired him to write the narrative, one of the first he wrote after moving to Concord. In the notebook he began after the wedding, he refers to himself and Sophia as Adam and Eve many times. In the tale he imagines that the Day of Doom has "burst upon the globe" and killed everyone on earth (10: 247). Everything else – all structures and physical objects – remain intact. Insofar as the narrative has a plot, it involves the new Adam and Eve walking around the Boston area and trying to interpret and understand the remains of civilization. This tour of the innocents enables Hawthorne to poke fun at various human institutions. Adam and Eve enter a church, but only a faint "odor of religion" lingers in the building (10: 252). They can't understand the purpose of a Court of Justice or a Hall of Legislature (10: 253), and they can't figure out the function of the gallows (10: 255). Entering a bank, they enable Hawthorne to satirize the materialism of nineteenth-century society; the money they see everywhere means nothing to them, and they consider it to be "rubbish" (10: 261). Hawthorne seems liberal and progressive as he judges the excesses of society from the vantage point of these innocent characters. But he seems rather conservative when he shows Adam and Eve instinctively identifying with certain stereotypical gender identities and roles. Eve handles a "fashionable silk" at a "dry-good store," and she puts it on "with the taste that nature moulded into her composition," showing herself off to Adam in a manner that gives him "his first idea of the witchery of dress" (10: 251). When Eve finds a woman's work-basket in a Beacon Street mansion, she "instinctively thrusts the rosy tip of her finger into a thimble" and "takes up a piece of embroidery" (10: 257). "Passing through a dark entry, they find a broom behind the door; and Eve, who comprises the whole nature of womanhood, has a dim idea that it is an instrument proper for her hand" (10: 258). In implying that a woman's identity and role are instinctive, Hawthorne forecloses upon possibilities that nineteenth-century feminists were raising – as in Margaret Fuller's famous declaration, "let them be sea-captains."[24] Several of the better-known tales Hawthorne wrote at the Old Manse suggest even more vexing views of women and of male–female relationships.

"The Birth-mark"

Despite early readings of "The Birth-mark" as a tale of failed idealism – readings that tend to ignore the fact that a man conducts experiments on his wife – the story features a sadistic male–female relationship that recalls Poe's "Ligeia" or "Berenice." Aylmer, the scientist-protagonist of "The Birth-mark," does not merely seek to perfect his wife Georgiana. Repelled by what he considers an imperfection in her appearance – a birthmark in the form of a miniature hand on her cheek – he subjects her to an early version of chemotherapy that kills her at the very moment that the mark itself disappears from her face. Judith Fetterley has argued that the story is a "brilliant analysis of the sexual politics of idealization." Georgiana epitomizes "woman as beautiful object, reduced to and defined by her body," and the story demonstrates that "the idealization of women has its source in a profound hostility toward women."[25] Brenda Wineapple has provocatively added that the story is "also a fantasy of abortion. The scientist kills his wife and what she produces so that he in some way can remain alone, untrammeled, asexual, and free from responsibility" (*Hawthorne* 175). From an artistic point of view, Aylmer also represents a Pygmalion or modern-day plastic surgeon, creating or recreating a woman as if she were a statue he is sculpting. At one point, he gives Georgiana such a deadly look that he changes "the roses of her cheek into a deathlike paleness, amid which the Crimson Hand was brought strongly out, like a bas-relief of ruby on the whitest marble" (10: 39). That red birthmark, signifier of a woman's embodied being, anticipates the scarlet letter on Hester's breast or the brands on dissenters' cheeks that Hawthorne noted in "Endicott and the Red Cross." With such emphasis on whiteness and on contamination of pure whiteness by another color (red, not black), "The Birth-mark" lends itself, like Poe's "Ligeia," to a racialized reading – illustrating a fixation in the white imagination on ensuring the purity of color and eradicating any hint of amalgamation. At one point, for example, Aylmer becomes so "startled with the intense glow of the birth-mark upon the whiteness of [Georgiana's] cheek that he could not restrain a strong convulsive shudder" (10: 43).

Whether read as a study of misogyny or racism, "The Birth-mark" illustrates the operation of the male imagination and the tendency to deform relationships and others by trying, in this case, to make a woman conform to the requirements of male desire. Anticipating the insights of feminist criticism and of readings such as Fetterley's, Hawthorne shows how even Georgiana herself becomes infected by the deforming tendency to see the birthmark as a flaw. Like contemporary women who have surgery in order to improve their appearance (according to male-identified standards), Georgiana "felt how much more precious was such a sentiment [Aylmer's love] than that meaner kind which would have borne with the imperfection for her sake, and have been guilty of treason to holy love by degrading its perfect idea to the level of the actual; and with her whole spirit she prayed that, for a single moment, she might satisfy his highest and deepest conception" (10: 52). Written in the early 1840s, shortly after the Trail of Tears culminated years of white efforts to displace and even exterminate Native Americans, shortly before the women's rights movement would gather momentum, "The Birth-mark" illustrates the consequences of eugenic efforts to perfect and purify race and gender characteristics.

"The Artist of the Beautiful"

Owen Warland, the protagonist in "The Artist of the Beautiful," deforms himself more than he injures Annie Hovenden, but he shares Aylmer's fixation on a single object of study that alienates him from others, especially from women. In Owen's case, the fixation is even more purely aesthetic. Instead of operating on a woman's body to make it perfect, Owen sublimates his feelings for Annie in an artistic quest to create ideal beauty – an intellectual quest that results in the creation of a beautiful mechanical butterfly. As Michael Davitt Bell puts it, Owen "protects himself from his own impulses through idealistic rationalization," but he is in fact "terrified by reality and especially by sex; he manages to escape into art and there express his repressed and guilty fantasies in the sublimated, rationalized form of artistic 'beauty.'"[26] Successful finally in his artistic pursuit, he is a failure in love; the child of Annie's marriage to the blacksmith Robert Danforth destroys Owen's beautiful mechanical butterfly. In addition to dramatizing a triangular relationship among Owen, Annie, and art, "The Artist of the Beautiful" also represents competing models of manhood, registering some of the anxiety Hawthorne felt after his marriage, as he turned to writing as a career.

In contrasting Owen Warland with Robert Danforth, Hawthorne represents two radically different male types that it is tempting to call the Fair Gentleman and Dark Male. In contrast to Danforth's "arm of might," Owen possesses a "delicate ingenuity." Taken once to see a steam engine, he

> turned pale, and grew sick, as if something monstrous and unnatural had been presented to him. The horror was partly owing to the size and terrible energy of the Iron Laborer; for the character of Owen's mind was microscopic, and tended naturally to the minute, in accordance with his diminutive frame and marvelous smallness and delicate power of his fingers.   (10: 450)

Warland and Danforth reflect the pressures Hawthorne felt most acutely during this period of his life to make money with his writing – to be a "writer for bread," as he told George Hillard (16: 23). But the men's very different characters also enable Hawthorne to contrast two types of creative and procreative power – relational and autogenetic (produced by the self alone).

Hawthorne meticulously traces the process by which Owen becomes an autogenetic creator, or "artist of the beautiful." Owen begins to consider Annie Hovenden a threat to his creative success, and he rejects the possibility of marriage in favor of lonely devotion to his art, laboring to give birth to art all by himself.[27] Although he persists in "connecting all his dreams of artistical success with Annie's image," his passion, Hawthorne says, "had confined its tumults and vicissitudes so entirely within the artist's imagination, that Annie herself had scarcely more than a woman's intuitive perception of it." Indeed, "in the aspect which she wore to his inward vision," Annie is "as much a creature of his own, as the mysterious piece of mechanism would be were it ever realized" (10: 464). With Annie's power married to his own (in his mind), Owen has the power to be the mother and father – the sole progenitor – of an artistic "child."

In the jewel-box "representing a boy in pursuit of a butterfly" (10: 469–70) that he gives Annie and Robert Danforth as a belated wedding present, Owen has replicated himself twice over – fathered a self onto a box that is "pregnant," as it were, with the butterfly-child he has fathered. When Annie asks him if the butterfly is alive, Owen replies like a proud father, "Alive? Yes, Annie; it may well be said to possess life, for it absorbed my own being into itself; and in the secret of that butterfly, and in its beauty – which is not merely outward, but deep as its whole system – is represented the intellect, the imagination, the sensibility, the soul, of an Artist of the Beautiful! Yes, I created it" (10: 471). The bliss of paternity that Owen feels is then confirmed by Danforth's envious comment, "That goes beyond me" (10: 472). In effect, Owen has proven a better father than the virile Danforth.

"Rappaccini's Daughter"

"Rappaccini's Daughter" (1844), like "The Birth-mark," tells the story of a young woman, Beatrice Rappaccini, who becomes the victim of a "mad" scientist – in this case, her father rather than her husband. Rappaccini ends up poisoning his daughter's system – making her poisonous – so that in order to save the young suitor, Giovanni Guasconti, whom her father has also poisoned, she drinks an antidote that kills her. The tale represents another of Hawthorne's acute psychological studies – an intense analysis of the male imagination in the process of coming to terms with a challenging woman. Like Goodman Brown or Robin Molineux, Giovanni is destined for an experience in which reason and imagination, consciousness and the unconscious, become confused. On the one hand he wants to bring Beatrice "rigidly and systematically within the limits of ordinary experience." On the other hand he is fascinated by the "wild vagaries which his imagination ran riot continually in producing" (10: 105).

Thomas Mitchell finds Margaret Fuller's presence throughout the tale and considers the story one of Hawthorne's major efforts to represent Fuller's meaning in his life. Mitchell argues that Hawthorne represented his relationship with both Emerson and Fuller in "Rappaccini's Daughter." Rappaccini's garden reflects Emerson's Concord circle. Dr. Rappaccini derives from Emerson himself: "Rappaccini creates and cultivates unnaturally beautiful and possibly poisonous plants (and a daughter–protégée) just as Emerson cultivates brilliant but possibly deluded insights and followers."[28] The acute tensions in the tale – especially the trauma that Beatrice provokes in Giovanni as he struggles to comprehend her and his feelings for her – derive for Mitchell from Hawthorne's similar efforts to find terms for his friendship with Fuller: "Hawthorne recognized within himself a sexual tension in his relationship with Fuller that threatened the 'brotherly' nature on which their relationship was founded and depended" (116).

Carol Bensick and Dawn Keetley also cite historical precedents for Beatrice's character, but they move further afield. Bensick's book-length study features a very convincing analysis of the sixteenth-century scientific Italian background of Hawthorne's tale. Most provocative is her argument, based on solid historical evidence, that Giovanni is the truly dangerous poisoner because he carries syphilis into Rappaccini's garden. Keetley finds a potential source much closer to home – a sensational Boston murder case in which Hannah Kinney was tried for poisoning her husband George. Keetley goes further, however, by arguing that Hawthorne's tale can be situated within a burgeoning market for sensational crime stories of which the Kinney case is only one real-life example.[29]

More fully than any other heroine in Hawthorne's tales, Beatrice Rappaccini exemplifies the sort of female vitality, passion, and self-expression that we associate with the heroines of his novels: Hester Prynne, Zenobia (*The Blithedale Romance*), and Miriam (*The Marble Faun*). Although deriving from the stereotype of the Dark Lady, none of these characters can be confined easily within expected roles, despite the concerted efforts of male characters and a male-dominated society to restrict them to a limited sphere. Beatrice possesses so much energy that she seems to be bursting with it. She "looked redundant with life, health, and energy," Hawthorne says; "all of which were bound down and compressed, as it were, and girdled tensely, in their luxuriance, by her virgin zone" (10: 97). Almost in spite of himself, Giovanni comes to view the girl as in some way essential to his own being: "The instant that he was aware of the possibility of approaching Beatrice, it seemed an absolute necessity of his existence to do so. It mattered not whether she were angel or demon; he was irrevocably within her sphere, and must obey the law that whirled him onward, in ever lessening circles, towards a result which he did not attempt to foreshadow" (10: 109). Young Goodman Brown and Robin Molineux experienced disorienting journeys in space that produced dream or nightmare visions. Giovanni's "journey" is psychological, and Hawthorne traces the imaginative process of that centripetal movement within his hero with remarkable precision.

Even though Beatrice warns Giovanni to believe nothing about her except what he can see with his own eyes (10: 111), Hawthorne once again dramatizes problems in perceiving reality – the clouding in this case of male perception by projection. Richard Brenzo argues that Giovanni is never entirely successful in liberating Beatrice from sexual stereotypes: "Swinging between the two classic extremes of viewing woman as demon or as saint, he never finds a basis in reality for his feelings about Beatrice."[30] Nonetheless, at selected moments Giovanni comes closer than his predecessors in Hawthorne's fiction to achieving a sympathetic, female-centered vision of a woman. He seems ready to act on Beatrice's own advice to forget "whatever you may have fancied in regard to me. If true to the outward senses, still it may be false in its essence. But the words of Beatrice Rappaccini's lips are true from the depths of the heart outward. Those you may believe" (10: 112). Beatrice is still more object than subject in this male-centered tale, but Hawthorne gives her some capacity to speak for herself.

Whereas Georgiana "learned to shudder" at Aylmer's gaze (10: 39) and gradually came to hate her birthmark (and herself) as much as he (10: 48), Beatrice more successfully maintains her integrity and even responds to Giovanni's "gaze of uneasy suspicion with a queenlike haughtiness" (10: 112). Whereas Georgiana accepted her appearance for Aylmer as her own reality, Beatrice demands the right to define herself in her own words. Momentarily Giovanni appears sensitive to such an outpouring from the heart. As a "fervor glowed in her whole aspect, and beamed upon Giovanni's consciousness like the light of truth itself," he "seemed to gaze through the beautiful girl's eyes into her transparent soul, and felt no more doubt or fear" (10: 112). Temporarily, Giovanni separates his image of Beatrice from the fear that she had provoked. "Whatever had looked ugly, was now beautiful; or, if incapable of such a change, it stole away and hid itself among those shapeless half-ideas, which throng the dim region beyond the daylight of our perfect consciousness" (10: 114). However hopeful this open, receptive stance may be, there is something ominous in the observation that Giovanni's initial impression of ugliness has hidden itself somewhere deep in his mind. Thoughts subject to such repression have a disturbing tendency to return to conscious life.

In fact, because Giovanni is finally unable to overcome his fears, he reneges on the relationship he has initiated. In failing to subordinate his anxiety to the "light of truth" with which Beatrice tries to define herself, he leaves her to the poisonous influence of her father. Hawthorne implies, even though he leaves the matter ambiguous, that Giovanni might have saved Beatrice from her father's poison if he had just had enough faith in her goodness. Though he still considers their meetings the "whole space in which he might be said to live" (10: 115), he will not touch what he views as poisonous. "At such times, he was startled at the horrible suspicions that rose, monster-like, out of the caverns of his heart, and stared him in the face; his love grew thin and faint as the morning-mist; his doubts alone had substance" (10: 116). His imagination is "incapable of sustaining itself at the height to which the early enthusiasm of passion had exalted it; he fell down, grovelling among earthly doubts, and defiled therewith the pure whiteness of Beatrice's image" (10: 120).

"Rappaccini's Daughter" is remarkable for the way it traces the operations of a man's imagination in the presence of a challenging woman. Hawthorne carefully delineates the process by which Beatrice is victimized by a man who cannot overcome his fears of woman. Giovanni cannot move beyond an essential narcissism – his assumption that Beatrice's role is to reflect an image of him. Thus, he fears the change in himself that an intimate relationship entails. When he contemplates the new self that his relationship with her has brought into being, he "grew white as marble, and stood motionless before the mirror, staring at his own reflection there, as at the likeness of something frightful" (10: 121). He becomes convinced that he has been infected by Beatrice's poison and feels transformed into a kind of statue by the frightening implications of what Beatrice reveals about himself.

Hawthorne's use of the mirror suggests another of those doublings back upon the self of the "horrible suspicions" which have risen out of the "caverns of the heart" – a perception of the self as other in which the thoughts previously projected upon Beatrice are now projected upon the self's own mirror-image. As Giovanni breathes upon a spider, which he finds suspended from the ceiling of his apartment, he seems to be exhaling his own evil thoughts about the girl. His breath is "imbued with a venomous feeling out of his heart" (10: 122). Soon afterwards, the venom from Giovanni's heart finds its way to his tongue; he speaks with "venomous scorn and anger" (10: 124). In an obvious example of projection, he accuses Beatrice of being the frightful object he fears himself to be. "Thou hast made me as hateful, as ugly, as loathsome and deadly a creature as thyself," he rages, "a world's wonder of hideous monstrosity!" (10: 124). Giovanni's accusation indicates his own fear of experience more than Beatrice's poisoned nature, and the final pages of the story link Giovanni with Rappaccini (and his mysterious rival, Baglioni) in a conspiracy against Beatrice. All three characters, according to Brenzo, "'project' upon Beatrice impulses they are unwilling to acknowledge as their own" (153). As Giovanni flirts with the idea that there might "still be a hope of his returning within the limits of ordinary nature, and leading Beatrice – the redeemed Beatrice – by the hand" (10: 125–26), Hawthorne observes his failure to recognize that, having "bitterly wronged" Beatrice's love, no hope of "earthly union and earthly happiness" remains (10: 126).

Not surprisingly, the process of projection, objectification, and scapegoating that marks Giovanni's experience lends itself to a racial interpretation. Anna Brickhouse notes that the story is obsessively concerned with questions of "unnatural reproduction" and hybrid plants, that Beatrice is "subtly coded as miscegenous herself" and thus a threat to racial purity that Hawthorne "locates in Giovanni."[31] Giovanni's fond hope that he can purify Beatrice, like Aylmer's wish to eliminate the red stain on Georgiana's white skin, situates the story within the white male imagination as a tale of racial profiling and eugenic purification. Whether intended or not, the tale betrays the concerns of many white Americans in the 1840s about the dangers of miscegenation and racial mixing.

Whether viewed as an illustration of racism or misogyny, "Rappaccini's Daughter" reveals the consequences for a woman of a man's failure to accept her as she is. Hawthorne himself demonstrates his keen interest in the male psychology he represents. Whether or not he would have considered Giovanni a racist or misogynist or simply a misguided and imaginatively limited youth, he clearly represents him as a failure. Even though the "mad scientists" (Rappaccini and Baglioni) are more directly to blame for Beatrice's fate, Giovanni is the object of her final words. Like Aylmer, Giovanni destroys Beatrice in the act of trying to save her – or at least a purified and objectified image of her. Hawthorne is typically ambiguous about whether Giovanni has actually been poisoned or has only introjected his fear of Beatrice and of relationship with her. In either case, Hawthorne plays a perverse joke on his protagonist and gives him a dose of his own medicine. By rejecting Beatrice and then, in effect, being rejected by her, Giovanni is condemned to take her place. In saving his life by drinking the deadly antidote first, Beatrice condemns him to live out his life, not exactly as a woman, but as her male double. Whether or not he remains in the garden, he must remain alone for fear of infecting another with the poison he believes he has absorbed.

"Drowne's Wooden Image"

Although Hawthorne uses the medium of woodcarving rather than writing, "Drowne's Wooden Image" (1844) represents his most explicit effort to explore a male artist's effort to create a female character. Hawthorne makes an obvious allusion to the Greek myth of Pygmalion and Galatea, in which Pygmalion sculpts a statue of a woman so beautiful that he falls in love with it. The goddess Venus takes pity on the sculptor and causes the statue to come to life, whereupon Pygmalion and Galatea marry and have a child. Hawthorne's version tells a different story – a story with an ambiguous appeal, it is tempting to speculate, for the readership of *Godey's Magazine and Lady's Book*, where it was first published in 1844.

Despite its startling verisimilitude, Drowne's carving lacks a "deep quality, be it of soul or intellect, which bestows life upon the lifeless, and warmth upon the cold, and which, had it been present, would have made Drowne's wooden image instinct with spirit" (10: 309). In Hawthorne's terms, Drowne hasn't achieved the power of a romancer because he is too concerned with being meticulously realistic. As he falls under the spell of a mysterious Portuguese woman, however, he becomes an "inspired artist" (10: 311). Instead of merely imposing an idea on a block of wood, Drowne surrenders his conscious designs to his medium and his model and seems to tap into deeper regions of his own psyche. "A well-spring of inward wisdom gushed within me," he confesses, "as I wrought upon the oak with my whole strength, and soul, and faith!" (10: 313). Indeed, no less an artist than John Singleton Copley, the most famous American painter of the eighteenth century, perfectly glosses the process which produced the wooden image: so powerful was the image of the woman, he suggests, that it "first created the artist who afterwards created her image" (10: 319). Hawthorne makes clear, moreover, that feelings of love sponsor this creative outburst, that the "expression of human love" is the "secret of the life that had been breathed into this block of wood" (10: 314). As Drowne himself says, "this work of my hands" is also the "creature of my heart" (10: 313). Drowne thus realizes an ideal that Hawthorne would define in his prefaces to *The Scarlet Letter* and *The House of the Seven Gables*; he expresses the truth of the human heart rather than the intentions of the intellect or conscious mind. Drowne also realizes an ideal that Hawthorne had expressed in his love letters to Sophia: a reciprocal relationship between the male artist and his female subject in which a woman's self-image brings a creative male self into being to form the work of art that embodies her. Drowne may be Pygmalion, but he does not seek creative and possessive power over a woman through his art. Rather, by surrendering control over the creative process, he becomes the agent or medium of a woman's self-creation. She creates herself through him.

Like most of Hawthorne's stories about art, however, "Drowne's Wooden Image" apparently ends unhappily. The "brief season of excitement, kindled by love" (10: 320) does not last. The Portuguese woman appears and, passing through Drowne's workshop, absorbs the life from his statue, leaving Drowne the "mechanical carver that he had been known to be all his lifetime" (10: 319). From Drowne's point of view, then, the story appears to end in failure. We can turn the tables on this conclusion, however, by considering the tale from the woman's point of view. Instead of being "killed into art" like Georgiana and Beatrice, the Portuguese woman retains her integrity and her vitality. Its "life" absorbed by the real woman, the statue "dies" instead, so from the woman's point of view, if not from Drowne's, the effect is a happy one. Indeed, the story can be read as a remarkably positive example of a woman's ability to enter the sphere of male art without sacrificing her power to be herself.

Chapter 4

Hawthorne's novels

The Scarlet Letter

For a writer who made no effort for twenty years to write another novel after the embarrassment he felt over *Fanshawe*, Hawthorne enjoyed surprising success when he finally returned to the novel form with *The Scarlet Letter*. Even in this case, however, the book that has become one of the two or three best-known nineteenth-century American novels began life as another short story. "The Custom-House," the preface Hawthorne added after completing the narrative, still includes several references to the collection in which he intended to include "The Scarlet Letter."

Published on 16 March 1850, *The Scarlet Letter* was a bestseller by nineteenth-century standards. The first edition of 2,500 copies sold out quickly, as did a second edition of 2,500 published a month later. (Ticknor and Fields published a third edition of 1,000 copies later in the year.) Hawthorne had been worried because his original intention was a collection of tales like *Mosses from an Old Manse*, and he feared that *The Scarlet Letter* was too short to make a book (one reason he added "The Custom-House" preface). He worried especially, as he told Fields, that the book would be too "somber" if comprised of only *The Scarlet Letter*. "I found it impossible to relieve the shadows of the story with so much light as I would gladly have thrown in. Keeping so close to its point as the tale does, and diversified no otherwise than by turning different sides of the same dark area to the reader's eye, it will weary very many people, and disgust some. Is it safe, then, to stake the fate of the book entirely on this one chance?" (16: 307). Hawthorne was willing to trust Fields's judgment, and he wasn't shy about offering his own marketing advice. "If 'The Scarlet Letter' is to be the title, would it not be well to print it on the title-page in red ink?" (16: 308). Fields did so, emphasizing the provocative aspects of the story that would attract and repel readers of the time. Hawthorne thought of the novel as "positively a h—ll-fired story" (16: 312).

Readers such as the Reverend Arthur Cleveland Coxe would have dropped the "positively." As Coxe would ask in an 1851 review, "Why has our author selected such a theme? Why, amid all the suggestive incidents of life in a wilderness . . . should the taste of Mr. Hawthorne have preferred as the proper material for romance, the nauseous amours of a Puritan pastor, with a frail creature of his charge, whose mind is represented as far more debauched than her body?"[1] Coxe worried especially that the novel signaled a trend in American novel publishing – that a "running undertide of filth" was becoming "requisite to a romance," that the "French era" had actually "begun in our literature." He felt sure that the novel "had done not a little to degrade our literature, and to encourage social licentiousness" (259). Hawthorne would have the last word for posterity; for when Fields told him about Coxe's review, he asked to see it if it is "really good." "I think it essential to my success as an author, to have some bitter enemies" (16: 387). It is tempting to think that the Reverend Coxe's condemnation of the novel helped Hawthorne to sell more copies.

The Scarlet Letter is still a provocative book. Even readers who haven't read it know about scarlet letters. Hawthorne has given us a way of thinking about crime and punishment – about the psychology of punishment and the desire we have to know the truth of guilt or innocence with a certainty that warrants such capital (letter) punishment. The Scarlet Letter is a novel about letters and their meaning and their effect. "What does the scarlet letter mean?" Pearl keeps asking, and Hawthorne certainly keeps that question in front of us throughout the novel. He also plays with the fact that the phrase, "the scarlet letter," refers to both the piece of cloth Hester wears on her dress and to the book we are reading. Efforts to read and interpret the scarlet letter, which recur throughout the novel, mirror our own efforts to interpret The Scarlet Letter.

Hawthorne introduces the problem of interpretation in "The Custom-House," the preface he wrote when the novel was almost finished. Pretending to discover a scarlet letter, as well as an account of Hester's story, in a storage room at the Custom House, he provides a lengthy account of his efforts to understand what the letter means. In the process, he gives us directions for reading the novel. When first perceived, the letter appears to be only a "certain affair of fine red cloth, much worn and faded." Already Hawthorne is playing with "A" words. He then notes that there were "traces about it of gold embroidery," which he recognizes as wonderfully skillful needlework. No two needle-workers stitch the same, of course, and Hawthorne has to consult some experts – "ladies conversant with such mysteries" – to learn more about this "now forgotten art." Another "A" word – "A" for Art.

Furthermore, in referring the letter to knowledgeable "ladies," Hawthorne clearly identifies the scarlet letter and its "art" with women, suggesting that women comprise the best audience for Hester's story because they are already "conversant" with its meaning. Indeed, Hawthorne underscores the point when he has a group of Puritan women form the first reading group for Hester's gold-embroidered A. "'She hath good skill at her needle, that's certain,' remarked one of the female spectators; 'but did ever a woman, before this brazen hussy, contrive such a way of showing it! Why, gossips, what is it but to laugh in the faces of our godly magistrates, and make a pride out of what they, worthy gentlemen, meant for a punishment?'" (1: 54). The women, Hawthorne implies, are in much better positions to recognize the transgressive power of Hester's embroidery – its power already to subvert intended meanings. What Hawthorne hints at in this scene is a double-tongued discourse in which Hester as artist works with existing language but changes its meaning through embroidery. Women get the point because they occupy the same position – a point Hawthorne makes clearer when he notes the sixth sense Hester develops, enabling her to know when another woman is looking empathetically at the scarlet letter. Hester goes on, as noted, to make her living through her needlework, her skill at which the scarlet letter itself advertises. "By degrees, nor very slowly," Hawthorne notes, "her handiwork became what would now be termed the fashion" (1: 82). Hester continues, however, to indulge herself – her self-expression – in her art. Although she does spend much of her time "making coarse garments for the poor," she makes more extravagant things, too. "She had in her nature a rich, voluptuous, Oriental characteristic, – a taste for the gorgeously beautiful, which, save in the exquisite productions of her needle, found nothing else, in all the possibilities of her life, to exercise itself upon" (1: 83).

Meanwhile, back at the Custom House. This "rag of scarlet cloth," as Hawthorne now calls it, "on careful examination, assumed the shape of a letter. It was the capital letter A." Hawthorne begins to sound passive, as if the letter had a mind and purpose of its own, while he can only watch it metamorphosize. Reasserting control, he determines to measure the letter, and he seems pleased to note that "each limb proved to be precisely three inches and a quarter in length." How absurd. Measuring the letter, like measuring a book, won't help us much in understanding. Hawthorne seems to recognize that, too, for he notes immediately that the letter "had been intended, there could be no doubt, as an ornamental article of dress; but how it was to be worn, or what rank, honor, and dignity, in by-past times, were signified by it, was a riddle which . . . I saw little hope of solving." Hawthorne's language – "intended," "signified" – suddenly starts to resonate. He is writing about reading and interpretation. He is misinterpreting, of course, but we recognize what he's about. "My eyes fastened themselves upon the old scarlet letter," he continues, "and would not be turned aside. Certainly, there was some deep meaning in it, most worthy of interpretation, and which, as it were, streamed forth from the mystic symbol, subtly communicating itself to my sensibilities, but evading the analysis of my mind" (1: 31). This is familiar territory. "Deep meaning," "interpretation," "mystic symbol" – all key terms in the practice of critical analysis.

The key idea, however, resides in the distinction between "sensibilities" and "mind." Again, Hawthorne casts himself in a passive position; the letter is active. Its meaning resists ordinary analytical methods. The letter's "deep meaning" communicates directly to a lower layer of understanding – sensibility. Feeling is involved, as well as reason. Indeed, understanding depends upon sympathetic identification, for in his final effort to understand the letter's deep meaning, he places it upon his breast. "It seemed to me," he tells us, "that I experienced a sensation not altogether physical, yet almost so, as of burning heat; and as if the letter were not of red cloth, but red-hot iron. I shuddered, and involuntarily let it fall upon the floor" (1: 32).

A remarkable passage and sequence of events – culminating in the reader's identifying with Hester Prynne by putting himself in her position, wearing the scarlet letter for all to see and interpret. Accurate "reading," Hawthorne seems to say, requires identification – a surrender of reason and ego-driven analysis, a creative passivity we associate with the Romantic movement in England and America. But I have glossed over the most striking feature of Hawthorne's sympathetic identification – his inability to sustain it. He drops the letter, which is too hot to handle, refusing to maintain his identification with Hester Prynne. His point is made, however. Don't think you can interpret the deep meaning of a letter – or a novel – unless you are willing to put yourself imaginatively in the position, here at least, of a woman. Put the red-hot letter on your own breast and see if you can stand the heat.

In addition to the "affair of red cloth," Hawthorne claims he found a "small roll of dingy paper," around which the letter had been twisted. The paper includes an account of Hester's life, especially her later years, when she works as a "voluntary nurse," doing "whatever miscellaneous good she might," and taking upon herself to "give advice in all matters, especially those of the heart." For her pains, "she gained from many people the reverence due to an angel" (1: 32). Hawthorne continues to have fun with "A" words – "affair," "advice," "angel" – the last of these words critical because as he introduces Hester to us with this term, we realize that it is the last term to characterize her. After seven years of wearing the letter and being branded an Adultress, we shall learn, many of the townspeople "refused to interpret the scarlet A by its original signification. They said that it meant Able, so strong was Hester Prynne, with a woman's strength" (1: 61). After Hester returns from England at the end of the novel and settles into the life Hawthorne reads about in Surveyor Pue's papers, the letter and Hester change meaning again – to "Angel." In a novel so concerned with not just what letters mean, but how they mean, these changes are significant. Hawthorne does not suggest that letters can mean anything we want them to mean. Hester's attempt to cast the letter off in the forest renders her unrecognizable to Pearl, who after all is identified with the letter. Hester cannot declare that the letter means nothing. That would be to deny the force and influence of history. Hawthorne is no strict constructionist, however. The scarlet letter is a living document whose meaning can change over time.

What *does* the scarlet letter mean? Most obviously, it means "Adultress," even though the word never appears in the text. The Puritans certainly feel confident that they have unmistakably identified Hester as exactly what she is – an Adultress, with a capital and scarlet A. But what happens almost immediately? "On the breast of her gown, in fine red cloth, surrounded with an elaborate embroidery and fantastic flourishes of gold thread, appeared the letter A" (1: 53). Hester has embroidered the scarlet letter – italicized it, revised it to become her own self-expressive signifier. Adultress? That's with a capital A, she seems to boast. Hester actually seems to be proud of what she has done. The Puritans get the point. As noted, they see Hester as laughing in the faces of the "godly magistrates" and making "a pride" out of what they meant for "a punishment." Hawthorne has fun in playing with "P" words in this passage. Can a punishment really be effective if the person being punished takes pride in what she has done? The answer – one that Anne Hutchinson gave in the seventeenth century and many early American feminists gave in the nineteenth century – is that society may have the power to punish behavior, but it cannot prevent women from believing that their behavior is right. At the same time, Hawthorne also seems to recognize that authors – those who put letters on paper or on people – cannot control the meaning of their works. When read by others, letters may have drastically different meanings from those their authors intended.

Later, in one of the most radical statements to appear in a nineteenth-century American novel, Hester tells Dimmesdale, "What we did had a consecration of its own. We felt it so! We said so to each other!" (1: 195). She doesn't care what people think. She doesn't care what the laws are. Not only that, she claims the right to consecrate – make holy – her own actions. And where do those actions come from? "We felt it so!" They come from feelings. We felt that what we did was not only right, but sacred. "We said so to each other!" Even this late in the novel – seven years after she exits her prison cell – Hester takes pride in what the magistrates intended for a punishment. It is no wonder that the meaning of the scarlet letter changes over time from Adultress to Able. Hester doesn't let the red-hot letter fall upon the ground; she embroiders it and wears it proudly. What does it stand for? Well, a lot of things – Adultress, Able, Angel, but also Arthur, as in Arthur Dimmesdale. What an irony. For seven years, while the Puritans seek to discover who fathered Hester's child, she is wearing his initial on her breast. When we consider that the Puritans sometimes made adulterers wear the letters "AD" on their breast to signify their crime, we appreciate Hawthorne's irony even more. If Hester Prynne had "AD" on her breast, would the Puritans have made the connection with Arthur Dimmesdale? Probably not. The ingenuity of this little trick: AD – AD ulterer – Arthur Dimmesdale.

Hawthorne also interests himself in *how* letters and other literary texts come to have meaning. Who defines the meaning of letters and texts? The issue is always before us, as case after case before the US Supreme Court makes clear. Hawthorne's novel represents one of the great literary efforts to explore the complexities of how letters have meaning. Even examining what the scarlet letter means is not just an abstract, semiotic exercise, for the Puritans do not simply intend to signify a crime with the letter A. They intend to brand a woman and thus identify her forever. *The Scarlet Letter* tells a human story, from Hester's point of view, of what it means to be branded and identified by others. Hester's bravado in embroidering the letter and declaring her act of adultery "consecrated" masks the agony she experiences almost daily. She may claim the power to create herself in advising Dimmesdale, for example, to "give up this name of Arthur Dimmesdale, and make thyself another, and a high one" (1: 198), but Hawthorne makes it clear that individual identity is negotiated between individuals and society and not so easily changed according to the individual's desire. In the opening scene of the novel, as Hester stands upon the scaffold, she retraces the path of her personal history – a foundation for identity – but then she looks down at the child she carries and at the letter on her breast: "these were her realities, – all else had vanished!" (1: 59). The Puritans' punishment has temporarily obliterated Hester's identity and given her a new one – an identity for them and thus for her. Hawthorne recognized that societies have such power.

The scarlet letter is not the only "document" whose meaning must be interpreted. Hawthorne also illustrates the susceptibility of human speech to be manipulated and misinterpreted. The opening scene of the novel, in which the Reverend Wilson urges Dimmesdale to "exhort" Hester to give up the father of her child to Puritan justice, offers a brilliant example of double meaning. The first-time reader, of course, occupies the same position as the Puritans – in no position to recognize the hidden meaning in Dimmesdale's speech. Clearly, speech acts do not exist in a vacuum or express meanings that are solely a function of the words being spoken.[2] To understand most speeches, we need a context – some prior message that clarifies meaning. We also need to know the context in which words are spoken and the relationship between the speaker and listener.

Called upon to convince Hester to reveal her lover's name – ironically, because he knows her "natural temper" better than anyone else (1: 65) – Dimmesdale faces the first of many conflicts between his private self and his public role. His solution to the problem, however, is as ingenious as it is dangerous: feeling divided in himself, he divides his "tongue" by insinuating a private message to Hester into his public speech. Although Hawthorne notes that Dimmesdale's speech "seemed" so powerful that people expect either Hester to "speak out the guilty name" or her lover to feel "compelled to ascend the scaffold" (1: 67–68), close attention to Dimmesdale's words makes obvious why neither event occurs. To begin, Dimmesdale alerts Hester to the "accountability" (another "A" word!) under which he labors, tacitly inviting her to discount what he says because of the external pressures on him to say it. Furthermore, he carefully designs the appeal itself to give her several reasons not to talk. As Michel Small has argued, by making his "charge" conditional, Dimmesdale thwarts its ostensible purpose.[3] "If thou feelest it to be for thy soul's peace, and that thy earthly punishment will thereby be made more effectual to salvation," he tells her, "I charge thee to speak out the name of thy fellow-sinner and fellow-sufferer!" (1: 67).

By not speaking out Dimmesdale's name, Hester gains power over him – power she saves for later use.[4] The opportunity comes after three years when she visits the Governor's Hall to plead with the magistrates not to remove Pearl from her custody. Because of Hester's marginal status, her pleas to the magistrates fall on deaf ears. Hawthorne clearly understood that words have meaning according to the political and social standing of the speaker. Hester recognizes this political reality, too, and quickly turns to Dimmesdale, whose power she has played a role in establishing and protecting, to speak for her:

> "Thou wast my pastor, and hadst charge of my soul, and knowest me better than these men can. I will not lose the child! Speak for me! Thou knowest, – for thou hast sympathies which these men lack! – thou knowest what is in my heart, and what are a mother's rights, and how much the stronger they are, when that mother has but her child and the scarlet letter! Look thou to it! I will not lose the child! Look to it!"
>
> (1: 113)

Hester understands how to speak doubly as well as Dimmesdale, and the minister, and any reader who has figured out their true relationship, understands the not-so-subtle secret message intended just for him – the implicit threat of exposure if he does not defend her. Three times Hester stresses how well Dimmesdale "knowest" her; she emphasizes that he "hadst charge" of her soul, that he has "sympathies" that the others lack, and especially that he alone knows what is in her heart. As if that weren't enough, she points out that she has only Pearl and the scarlet letter – no husband or partner, no help whatever from this "dead-beat" dad.

Dimmesdale gets the point, for he leaps to his task, lending his authority to the words Hester has spoken by echoing her speech. Much like the strategy of having slave narratives (for example, Frederick Douglass's) introduced and authenticated by white abolitionists (William Lloyd Garrison and Wendell Phillips), Hester relies on Dimmesdale's position not so much to make the case for her as to validate the case she has made. Where she had acknowledged Pearl's twofold effect (as her "happiness" and "torture"), he begins by remarking, "there is truth in what she says" (1: 113) and then confirms Pearl's dual effect as a "blessing" and a "torture" (1: 113, 114). Dimmesdale's speech has the intended effect – Hester's intended effect – as the magistrates reconsider their decision and allow Hester to keep Pearl. Hester has learned how to work the men and the system that keep her virtually powerless.

The Scarlet Letter is much more subtle than "The Minister's Black Veil" in its treatment of a minister who hides his true self from others. The use of an actual black veil in the short story gives way to an invisible veil in the novel. Most interestingly, Hawthorne explores the psychology of such veiling – the psychology of hypocrisy. "Canst thou deem it, Hester, a consolation," Dimmesdale says in the forest scene, "that I must stand up in my pulpit, and meet so many eyes turned upward to my face, as if the light of heaven were beaming from it! – must see my flock hungry for the truth, and listening to my words as if a tongue of Pentecost were speaking! – and then look inward, and discern the black reality of what they idolize? I have laughed, in bitterness and agony of heart, at the contrast between what I seem and what I am!" (1: 191). Even in this admission, Dimmesdale fools himself. He ignores his own responsibility for the false interpretation that his hungry flock places upon his words.

The Scarlet Letter offers a brilliant analysis of group psychology – of the way, to use Dimmesdale's term, a "hungry" group of people will believe what they want and need to believe about a public figure, regardless of the evidence before their eyes. That is, Hawthorne clearly understood the political dimensions of truth – the way "truth" is always negotiated between speakers and listeners, even when the "light of heaven" seems to be "beaming" forth from the speaker. Witness the final scene, after Dimmesdale has bared his chest to his parishioners and seemingly confessed his identity as adulterer and father of Pearl. Many people in the audience hear no confession, see no scarlet letter on their minister's chest. We "must be allowed to consider this version of Mr. Dimmesdale's story," Hawthorne writes, "as only an instance of that stubborn fidelity with which a man's friends – and especially a clergyman's – will sometimes uphold his character; when proofs, clear as the mid-day sunshine on the scarlet letter, establish him a false and sin-stained creature of the dust" (1: 259). Dimmesdale at one point tells his congregation, "I, whom you behold in these black garments of the priesthood . . . I, your pastor, whom you so reverence and trust, am utterly a pollution and a lie" (1: 143). As Hawthorne comments, "Could there be plainer speech than this? Would not the people start up in their seats, by a simultaneous impulse, and tear him down out of the pulpit which he defiled? Not so, indeed! They heard it all, and did but reverence him the more" (1: 144).

Modern readers think the townspeople fools, although there are plenty of modern examples of congregants refusing to believe ill of their philandering pastors. Hawthorne knew his psychology, especially his Puritan psychology, and knew, as the hypocritical Dimmesdale must have known, that such confessions of sinfulness were expected and appreciated. "The godly youth!" say his parishioners among themselves. "The saint on earth! Alas, if he discern such sinfulness in his own white soul, what horrid spectacle would he behold in thine or mine!" (1: 144). In fact, Hawthorne tells us point blank that Dimmesdale knows what he is doing. "The minister well knew – subtle but remorseful hypocrite that he was," Hawthorne tells us, "the light in which his vague confession would be viewed." He knows that his hungry hearers will praise him for appearing to put the scarlet letter on his own chest. He's a hypocrite and he knows that of himself. Therefore, Hawthorne concludes, "he loathed his miserable self" (1: 144). The psychology of hypocrisy remains a current topic.

More than any other character in the novel – more than even Roger Chillingworth – little Pearl keeps Dimmesdale's hypocrisy front and center before the reader. Hawthorne makes Pearl a kind of one-woman chorus, who asks repeatedly what the scarlet letter means and why the minister keeps his hand over his breast. Why would Hawthorne choose Pearl for this role? In part, perhaps, because he wants to play upon the romantic bias toward children's innocence. More important, Pearl is intimately identified with the letter; she is the "scarlet letter in another form; the scarlet letter endowed with life!" (1: 102). Hester even dresses her to resemble the letter, effectively embroidering Pearl, as she had embroidered the letter, to flaunt the child in front of the Puritans. In asking what the letter means, Pearl asks about herself and her origins – about her own meaning and being in the world. In addition, Hawthorne notes that "mother and daughter stood together in the same circle of seclusion from human society" (1: 94), reminding us that *The Scarlet Letter* tells the tale of a broken family. One of the reasons that the novel resonates so strongly for us still is its depiction of what is today an all-too-common family configuration – single mother, dead-beat dad, conflicted child.

Hawthorne's description and use of Pearl are all the more remarkable when we consider that, although Pearl seems to be a realistic portrait of a Puritan child, the "elf-child," as Hawthorne calls her, was based on his own daughter, Una. Hawthorne kept a detailed journal about his children's development, and he transferred some of the passages he wrote about Una directly into *The Scarlet Letter*. There "is something that almost frightens me about the child," he wrote about his daughter; "I know not whether elfish or angelic, but, at all events, supernatural ... I now and then catch an aspect of her, in which I cannot believe her to be my own human child, but a spirit strangely mingled with good and evil, haunting the house where I dwell" (8: 430–31). In *The Scarlet Letter* Hawthorne notes that Pearl possesses a "look so intelligent, yet inexplicable, so perverse, sometimes so malicious, but generally accompanied by a wild flow of spirits, that Hester could not help questioning, at such moments, whether Pearl was a human child. She seemed rather an airy sprite." "Thou art not my child! Thou art no Pearl of mine!" says Hester (1: 98). In his notebook Hawthorne observed the "evil spirit that struggles for mastery of [Una]; he is not a spirit at all, but an earthy monster, who lays his grasp on her spinal marrow, her brain, and other parts of her body that lie in closest contiguity to her soul; so that the soul has the discredit of these evil deeds" (8: 420–21). In the novel Hester fancies that she sees "another face in the small black mirror of Pearl's eye. It was a face, fiend-like, full of smiling malice . . . It was as if an evil spirit possessed the child, and had just peeped forth in mockery" (1: 97). In view of Hawthorne's conflicted reactions to Una, it is tempting to see his representation of the Puritans' and especially Arthur Dimmesdale's efforts to come to terms with Pearl as having a biographical source.

When Dimmesdale holds hands with Hester and Pearl on the scaffold in chapter 12, the three form an "electric chain," and the minister feels a "tumultuous rush of new life, other life than his own, pouring like a torrent into his heart, and hurrying through all his veins, as if the mother and the child were communicating their vital warmth to his half-torpid system" (1: 153). In this powerful passage, Hawthorne reveals both the cost of estrangement and the potential for rebirth that family represents. This is not to disparage the force of Hester's single motherhood, for Hawthorne certainly demonstrates the effectiveness of her parenting.

From the Puritans' point of view, however, Pearl is an illegitimate child who has no place in society. She is one of the "children of the Lord of Misrule" (1: 109), a subversive force associated with witchcraft and the wilderness. She has been scapegoated with her mother, the two of them exiled to the margins. Pearl, however, has a centripetal force of character. She keeps trying to find a place for herself in the community.[5] Indeed, her integration into the bosom of the community is essential not only for her discovery of an identity and social role, but also for the community's collective health. Instinctively, Pearl seems to know that Dimmesdale holds the key to her place. Pearl's most important role in the novel is to embody the future of Puritan society, the accommodation of society and the wilderness, the inside with the outside. Just as Dimmesdale must finally acknowledge her, thereby acknowledging the wholeness of his own divided nature, the Puritan community must acknowledge and confirm the legitimacy of those passions (associated with the forest, the Indian, the nature of women, the creative forces of the unconscious) which it has denied and repressed. In the forest, for example, Pearl encourages Hester and Dimmesdale to make a public demonstration of their relationship and of her identity as their daughter. Just as she will not accept Dimmesdale's "mockery of penitence" (1: 148) in the midnight privacy of the scaffold, she will not accept her parents' escapist indulgence in the freedom of the forest. She stands estranged from both of them across the brook, on the other side of the "boundary between two worlds" (1: 208). Pearl and the letter are symbolically one, so in casting off the letter, Hester rejects Pearl. By reaffixing the letter to her bosom, Hester preserves the only context in which Pearl can have her being: an environment in which the meaning of the letter and the child are continually before the public eye. Not by escaping the implications of the letter, but by acknowledging its full meaning, Pearl seems to say, can any of them realize their full human potential and assimilate that meaning into the imaginative life of the future.

Hawthorne's portrait of Arthur Dimmesdale as a failed father would have resonated for nineteenth-century readers. Dimmesdale's obvious conflict between his ministerial job and his unacknowledged family responsibilities make him a parody of the "absent" father, who was becoming increasingly common in nineteenth-century America, as men's work moved out of the home. Dimmesdale's portrait also derives from anxieties Hawthorne felt about being both a writer and a father. When Hawthorne wrote *The Scarlet Letter*, he was a father twice over, and his notebook entries clearly evidence great joy in his paternal role.[6] And as a writer who wrote at home, he was not the typical absent or distant father. As Sophia admitted, "Every mother is not like me – because not every mother has such a father for her children; so that my cares are forever light."[7] Becoming a father made Hawthorne think about writing in a different way, however. He felt a conflict between being a writer and being a father–provider. "God keep me from ever being really a writer for bread!" he told George Hilliard. "If I alone were concerned, I had rather starve; but in that case, poor little Una would have to take refuge in the alms-house which, here in Concord, is a most gloomy old mansion. Her 'angel face' would hardly make a sunshine there" (16: 23). Being such a writer, he recognized, meant entering the world as writer–businessman and thus producing a different kind of writing. "It will never do for me to continue merely a writer of stories for the magazines – the most unprofitable business in the world," he reasoned. "If I am to support myself by literature, it must be by what is called drudgery, but which is incomparably less irksome, as a business, than imaginative writing – by translation, concocting of school-books, newspaper-scribbling, &c" (16: 23).

Hawthorne's depiction of Dimmesdale's attitude toward Pearl makes *The Scarlet Letter* a compelling case study of the psychology and the ethos of nineteenth-century American fatherhood. Examined in light of various advice books of the period, especially Henry Clarke Wright's *Marriage and Parentage*, published only four years later, the novel entered an ongoing nineteenth-century dialogue about parentage and, especially, about a father's biological, psychological, and moral responsibilities to his children.

In *Marriage and Parentage* Wright provides a frank discussion of human sexuality, as well as marital and parental responsibilities. His "great end," he admits, is to "create a conscience in men and women, as to the use of their sexual element and relations," in order to "bring the sexual element under the government of an enlightened reason and a tender conscience."[8] As much as echoing Hawthorne's claim in *The Scarlet Letter* that the "very nature of the opposite sex" (men) must be "essentially changed, before woman can be allowed to assume what seems a fair and suitable position" (1: 165), Wright argues that a "new type of Manhood and Womanhood must precede the new type of Society" (20). Men especially must "control all their passional expressions," lest they do irreparable damage to their wives and children. Otherwise, women will "fear" the "passion of their husbands" and communicate that fear, with disastrous and even deforming results, to their children (100).

Hawthorne addresses many of these issues in *The Scarlet Letter*, most directly in the scene at the Governor's house. In explaining to Governor Bellingham and the other patriarchs why Hester should be allowed to keep Pearl, Dimmesdale subtly denies his fatherhood, disclaiming responsibility for Pearl's birth by shifting it to God, the "Heavenly Father." "This child of its father's guilt and its mother's shame," he maintains, "hath come from the hand of God, to work in many ways upon her heart, who pleads so earnestly, and with such bitterness of spirit, the right to keep her." In echoing Hester's claim that Pearl is both a "blessing" and a "torture" (1: 114), he argues backwards from effect to cause in order to exonerate himself. For if Pearl came from the "hand of God" to work upon Hester's heart, Dimmesdale himself was God's agent, as if, by impregnating Hester and denying his responsibility, he were doing God's work. Dimmesdale's argument is an obvious rationalization, but it assumes new dimensions in the context of ongoing debates in nineteenth-century America about sex education and the question of origins, a debate that for both Hawthorne and Wright focused on the catechism.

Earlier in this scene, the Reverend Wilson had interrogated Pearl about who "made" her, and even though she is well versed in the New England Primer and the Westminster Catechism, Pearl perversely answers that "she had not been made at all, but had been plucked by her mother off the bush of wild roses, that grew by the prison-door" (1: 112). The expected answer is that God made her. Remarkably, Wright duplicated this scene in *Marriage and Parenthood* in order to criticize the catechism for not telling children the truth about their biological origins. Indeed, Wright includes a conversation between a teacher and a little girl, "some three years old, of whom the teacher asked – 'Jane, who made you?'" Like Pearl (three years old in the scene at the Governor's Hall), Jane replies that she "grew on a rose bush" (Wright, 117). And like the Reverend Wilson, the child's teacher considers her answer "Dreadful," the result of parental neglect. The visitor who witnessed the interrogation, however, is more shocked by the teacher's reaction than by Jane's answer. Why not tell the child that she "derives existence from the parents?" he argues. "When you say to that child, 'GOD MADE YOU,' your words convey to her mind an untruth, as really as do the words of her mother, when she says she grew on a rose bush" (Wright, 118). Wright's conclusions about the scene his visitor has witnessed seem uncannily aimed at Hawthorne. Indeed, if the Reverend Wright had been in the Reverend Wilson's place, he would have responded very differently to Pearl's answer. For Wright, there was no "neutral territory" between the "real world" and "fairy-land" – at least not when it came to educating children about sexuality and reproduction. Romance, in his view, was falsehood. Veiling the actual facts of procreation – pretending that children came from "fairy-land" – was irresponsible, because ignorant or misguided children were likely to become sexually and parentally irresponsible adults.

> Thus, in the first step of what is called a religious education, children, instead of being directed to known *facts*, are led off into the regions of romance; and a fiction is presented to them as a fact. Instead of directing their minds to realities, which would, generally, satisfy their curiosity, and set them at rest on the rock of truth, they are sent off into the world of fancy, in search of one to whom they owe existence. From this false starting-point, they are led on, step by step, into the dark, intricate ways of an infinite romance, until they lose sight of the facts of their being, and are prepared to receive as literal truth, the most absurd and monstrous fictions. It is cruel thus to abuse the minds of children, when they so much more readily apprehend facts than fiction, and appreciate truth than falsehood. An untruth is ever hurtful to the human soul.   (118)

The ethics of parenting, as well as the question of what is best for Pearl, is precisely the issue in the scene at the Governor's Hall. "It is a flagrant violation of the law of parentage," Wright maintained, "for a man and woman to give existence to children they cannot or will not care for, and leave them to the care of strangers and asylums" (77). While Hester vehemently asserts her right to care for Pearl, Dimmesdale wants nothing to do with raising his child and obviously fails Pearl as a parent. "God gave her the child," he argues, "and gave her, too, an instinctive knowledge of its nature and requirements . . . which no other mortal being can possess." In arguing for the existence of a maternal, but no paternal, instinct, Dimmesdale excuses himself from parental responsibility, as if it would not be right to intrude himself upon what he calls the "awful sacredness in the relation between this mother and this child" (1: 114). In that claim, he is clearly at odds with nineteenth-century beliefs that paternal, as well as maternal, influences were crucial to child development. "What greater crime can a man commit," asks Wright, "than to give existence to a child that he cannot or *will not* care for? If any act should consign a man to infamy, this should" (127). Wright could certainly have Dimmesdale in mind when he condemns fathers who sacrifice their children for their own worldly success, but his comments also have an interesting bearing on the social world of *The Scarlet Letter* and on a society that rewards irresponsible fathers such as Dimmesdale with success. Men who abandon their offspring, Wright notes, "are often counted the highest ornaments of the church and of society, and elevated to the highest offices; while their children, and the mothers who bore them, are suffering in poverty and neglect. Of all earthly criminals, such are the most deserving condemnation" (127–28).

Hawthorne's difficulty in believing Una to be his "own human child" is magnified many times over in Dimmesdale who, for seven years, has dreaded the possibility that his paternity might be traced in his daughter's features. "Dost thou know, Hester," he says, "that this dear child, tripping about always at thy side, hath caused me many an alarm? Methought – O Hester, what a thought is that, and how terrible to dread it! – that my own features were partly repeated in her face, and so strikingly that the world might see them!" (1: 206). Hawthorne's "dread" of his family's suffering may have translated into Dimmesdale's "dread" that his features could be traced in Pearl's, but with Dimmesdale's portrait Hawthorne seemed, once and for all, to put his fears about fatherhood behind him. Even though he faced difficult choices during his years abroad between the suddenly incompatible roles of provider and nurturer, the older Hawthorne could take a much more balanced view of the difficulties of fatherhood. Indeed, looking back upon his earlier anxious moments, he could admit to Horatio Bridge (June 6, 1856) that, while he wished he were "a little richer,"

> when I compare my situation with what it was before the publication of the Scarlet Letter, I have reason to be satisfied with my run of luck. And, to say the truth, I had rather not be *too* prosperous;–it may be superstition, but it seems to me that the bitter is very apt to come with the sweet, and bright sunshine with a dark shadow; so I content myself with a moderate portion of sugar, and about as much sunshine as that of an English summer's day. In this view of the matter, I am disposed to thank God for the gloom and chill of my early life, in hope that my share of adversity came then, when I bore it alone, and that therefore it need not come now, when the cloud would involve those whom I love.
>
> (17: 497)

Hawthorne was still in England when he wrote this letter. He had not yet had to endure the agony of Una's near-fatal bout with Roman fever, which, he admitted in a notebook entry, "pierced into my very vitals" (14: 518). At the same time, the letter to Bridge suggests, it seems to me, that Hawthorne had solved the dilemma that he shared with other fathers. He had struck a difficult balance, at least in his own mind, between his roles as father and as provider. In his own terms, he had not only come to accept himself as an "Actual" (rather than "Imaginary" father), but his fatherhood had finally become that ideal "neutral territory" where sunshine and shadow, hope and fear, could meet and "each imbue itself with the nature of the other."

If Hawthorne raises the possibility of fulfilling such an ideal in *The Scarlet Letter*, he obviously falls short of its realization. Dimmesdale is overwhelmed by his experience in the forest and by the image of himself that it reveals. He conceives an alternative plan to the one he had made with Hester. Instead of sailing for Europe with her and Pearl, he will preach the Election Sermon, climaxing his career as a Puritan pastor, and then confess – or seem to confess – his sins, before going on to Heaven by himself. Once again, he leaves Hester and Pearl to fend for themselves. To be sure, Dimmesdale's public acknowledgement of Hester and Pearl is intended to validate their rightful places in the community and seems to create – momentarily – a kind of holy family to ensure the future. Pearl effectively consecrates this new relationship and seems to discover a new familial and social identity: "Pearl kissed his lips. A spell was broken. The great scene of grief, in which the wild infant bore a part, had developed all her sympathies; and as her tears fell upon her father's cheek, they were the pledge that she would grow up amid human joy and sorrow, nor for ever do battle with the world, but be a woman in it" (1: 256). If this were a movie, we would hear the swell of music, the promise of a rebirth, and see a fadeout to a glorious future.

The ending that Hawthorne wrote tells a mixed and ambiguous story. Pearl does apparently flourish, but in England rather than in Puritan America. Surprisingly, she inherits not from Dimmesdale, but from Chillingworth – making her the "richest heiress of her day, in the New World" (1: 261). She and Hester settle in England, where Pearl appears to marry well and have children for whom Hester, after her return to the colony, makes lavishly embroidered baby clothes (1: 262).

Perhaps the most controversial aspect of the ending for recent readers has been Hester's return and her resumption, "of her own free will," of the scarlet letter (1: 263). Given the radical strength she had displayed, especially in her forest declaration that her actions had a "consecration" of their own, given the self-reliant individualism she espouses when she urges Dimmesdale to invent a new name, Hester's resumption of her role as branded woman seems disappointing – a betrayal of her character's potential. As noted in chapter 2, critics such as Jean Fagan Yellin, Jonathan Arac, and Sacvan Bercovitch have emphasized Hawthorne's failure to allow Hester to fulfill her potential as a radical reformer and have linked the advice she gives women with the gradualist approach toward abolition and women's rights promoted by democrats such as Franklin Pierce. The 1995 movie version of *The Scarlet Letter*, directed by Roland Joffe and starring Demi Moore and Gary Oldman, ends with Hester, Dimmesdale, and Pearl riding off to North Carolina, casting the scarlet letter into the mud as they leave town. Hawthorne must have considered such an ending, although Rhode Island would make more sense as a destination in 1649 and would have enabled Hester to follow more precisely in the steps of Anne Hutchinson. Of course, in wishing for a different ending, we share a wish with Hawthorne himself, who was determined in his next novel to write a very different story – although a story with a "gingerbread" house destination that has proven too sweet for many readers' taste.

The House of the Seven Gables

Hawthorne wrote *The House of the Seven Gables* as an antidote to *The Scarlet Letter*. Even though he had bragged to James T. Fields that the ending of *The Scarlet Letter* had broken his wife's heart and "sent her to bed with a grievous headache" – a reader response that he termed a "triumphant success" (16: 311) – he wanted to write a different book. When he described Sophia's response to *The House of the Seven Gables*, he could brag that the book had "met with extraordinary success from that portion of the public to whose judgement it has been submitted; – viz, from my wife" (16: 386). Sophia's judgment seemed to influence Hawthorne's own view of the book, for he went on to say that he preferred the new novel to *The Scarlet Letter*. This is the same letter, however, in which he noted that he had heard about Arthur Cleveland Coxe's negative review of *The Scarlet Letter* and had stubbornly insisted that he didn't care, because it was "essential" to his success as an author to have "some bitter enemies" (16: 387).

There are many differences between *The Scarlet Letter* and *The House of the Seven Gables*. More than any other of his novels, *The House of the Seven Gables* seems attuned to the American present – engaged with various social, economic, and technological phenomena. The novel makes significant use of mesmerism and daguerreotypy, but it also features class conflicts, business and political intrigue, and a serious engagement with questions of gender identities and roles for both men and women.

Hepzibah Pyncheon's reluctant decision to open a cent shop because she desperately needs the money enables Hawthorne to engage the streets of Salem – to represent the street traffic that otherwise would never enter the aristocratic precincts of the House. Hepzibah feels embarrassed when she discovers that her customers "evidently considered themselves not merely her equals, but her patrons and superiors" (2: 54). After her first day on the job, this "decayed gentlewoman" (2: 54) comes to some "disagreeable conclusions as to the temper and manners of what she termed the lower classes, whom, heretofore, she had looked down upon with a gentle and pitying complacence, as herself occupying a sphere of unquestionable superiority." One of Hawthorne's purposes is to portray the social leveling forces at work in American society, coincident with the rise of business, manufacturing, and a host of opportunities to sell things, including entertainment, to increasingly wealthy middle-class people. Hepzibah, for example, quickly finds herself with a double identification. Suddenly a member of the shopkeeper's class, she looks with disdain at the "idle aristocracy" – at one woman in particular, whose "delicate and costly summer garb" and "slippered feet" make her look as if she is floating down the street. "For what good end," Hepzibah wonders bitterly, "in the wisdom of Providence, does that woman live! Must the whole world toil, that the palms of her hands may be kept white and delicate?" (2: 55).[9]

Even if the central focus of the novel remains the fortunes of the aristocratic Pyncheons, Hawthorne includes a working-class perspective – often in the form of characters who critique the Pyncheons from outside their house. Even before Hepzibah has her first customer, two "laboring men" assess her prospects (2: 47). Savvy patrons of local businesses, they don't think much of Hepzibah's chances. Jaffrey will later tell her that, ever since Clifford's return from prison, her "neighbors have been eye-witnesses to whatever passed in the garden. The butcher, the baker, the fishmonger, some of the customers of your shop, and many a prying old woman, have told me several of the secrets of your interior" (2: 236). This remarkable statement, which sounds more like something we would hear in our own time, is a function of social leveling. The street itself is a marketplace, furthermore, featuring vendors and popular entertainers. In a scene that Hawthorne took directly from his notebook, he describes an organ grinder and his monkey, who set up opposite the Pyncheon house to entertain the crowd.

With his "man-like expression" and "enormous tail, (too enormous to be decently concealed under his gabardine" (2: 164), the organ grinder's monkey has received special critical attention because of its sexual suggestiveness and racial characteristics. Hawthorne took this incident from his notebook and revised it in a few interesting ways. In both cases he emphasizes the sexuality of the monkey's tail, but in the novel he adds to his notebook passage the remark about the tail's sticking out from under the monkey's costume. On the other hand, he gives no evidence in the novel version (nor would we expect him to) that he was with Una when they saw the organ-grinder. "Una was with me, holding my forefinger, and walking decorously along the pavement," he recorded in his notebook. "She stopped to contemplate the monkey, and after a while, shocked by his horrible ugliness, began to cry" (8: 271). In the novel Hawthorne transfers Una's shock and tears to Clifford (2: 164).

Marked by "anthropomorphic signs of race, gender, and even sexuality," in David Anthony's words, the monkey "is only a thinly veiled caricature of a performative black masculinity, one that Hawthorne seems to have expected his readers to recognize."[10] Representative, too, of increasingly popular forms of mass entertainment, such as the minstrel show, the monkey "offers the sort of obscene caricature of black male sexuality so common within the period's minstrel performances" (Anthony, 447). The chapter ("The Arched Window") in which the organ-grinder appears is a set piece – an example of the crowd scenes that Hawthorne loved to write and an opportunity for him to root the House of the Seven Gables in the texture of popular culture.

For all of its embeddedness in nineteenth-century life, *The House of the Seven Gables* depends even more on the romance conventions, especially of character, that Hawthorne had already relied upon and would use again in subsequent novels. One of the most important differences between the novel and *The Scarlet Letter* resides in the difference between the heroines, Hester Prynne and Phoebe Pyncheon. In his later novels, Hawthorne would double his main female characters, resorting to the conventional contrast between dark and light women. Phoebe Pyncheon derives from the latter type, and bears the nickname, Phoebe, that Hawthorne used for Sophia. Although she possesses strength of character and purpose, Hawthorne relegates her influence to the domestic sphere. It is hard to imagine her in the forest making the radical declarations that Hester made there, and in one crucial scene, as we shall see, Hawthorne makes sure that she won't be in any danger of wearing a scarlet letter. In contrast to female characters who challenge social boundaries, Phoebe is contained and self-contained, a model of conformity. She is "orderly and obedient to common rules" (2: 68) and "shocked no canon of taste; she was admirably in keeping with herself, and never jarred against surrounding circumstances" (2: 80).

In fact, Phoebe purifies the space around her of anything unpleasant. Although her room in the Pyncheon house was once a "chamber of very great and varied experience" – births, deaths, and the "joy of bridal nights" that had "throbbed" away there – Phoebe transforms it into a "maiden's bed-chamber" that has been "purified of all former evil and sorrow by her sweet breath and happy thoughts" (2: 72). As Amy Schrager Lang puts it, Phoebe exhibits "all the virtues of middle-class femininity," and she is "imported from the domestic universe of works like *The Lamplighter* into the gothic world of the house of the seven gables just in time to avert the crisis of social classification prompted by her cousin Hepzibah's impoverishment. Phoebe's strategic arrival plays out in narrative form her larger ideological function," which is to mediate between the upper and lower classes.[11]

Holgrave, Hawthorne's hero, has the potential to be one of his most interesting male characters – a very different man from the pale Arthur Dimmesdale. Class conflict plays an important role in *The House of the Seven Gables* in the tension between the Pyncheons and the Maules, and Holgrave clearly comes from a workingman's background. "I was not born a gentleman," he insists to Hepzibah; "neither have I lived like one" (2: 45). He is the sort of man Hawthorne encountered on the docks in Boston and Salem when he worked in the Custom Houses there, and he resembles many of the Brook Farmers whose ranks Hawthorne seemed proud to join. Holgrave promises to be a spokesman for democratization and social leveling of the sort that the Brook Farmers imagined. The terms "lady" and "gentleman," he observes, "had a meaning, in the past history of the world, and conferred privileges, desirable, or otherwise, on those entitled to bear them. In the present – and still more in the future condition of society – they imply, not privilege, but restriction" (1: 45).

A man on the make, Holgrave also represents the new breed of entrepreneurial opportunists that proliferated in nineteenth-century America. In stark contrast to Hepzibah, who feels as if the "sordid stain" from the first copper coin she receives in her newly opened cent shop "could never be washed away from her palm" (1: 51), Holgrave seems comfortable in a society that increasingly valued and rewarded men who invested themselves in business and marketable professions. Protean in his capabilities – a far cry from the eighteenth-century model of artisanship and lifelong devotion to a single craft – he is only twenty-two years old but has already held many positions: country schoolmaster (like Melville's Ishmael in *Moby-Dick*), salesman, editor, peddler, dentist, mesmerist, and of course Daguerreotypist (2: 176). Holgrave has changed with the economy, taking up each new thing as it comes along and promises to turn a profit. Compared to the relatively shy and retiring Hawthorne, his talents seem modern. All of these positions require public performance and marketing ability – a willingness to put oneself before the public, to market oneself for money.

Most intriguingly, Holgrave purports to be a political and social reformer. Hepzibah notes that he "had the strangest companions imaginable" – "reformers, temperance-lecturers, and all manner of cross-looking philanthropists," "community-men and come-outers" (2: 84). In brief, Hepzibah concludes, "he has a law of his own" (2: 85) – a statement that recalls Hester Prynne's radicalism. Holgrave travels in radical circles. He has spent some time in a community of Fourierists (2: 176) – a philosophy that Brook Farm adopted after Hawthorne left – and he seems essentially utopian in his outlook. He had the "sense, or inward prophecy," Hawthorne notes, to believe that

> we are not doomed to creep on forever in the old, bad way, but that, this very now, there are the harbingers abroad of a golden era, to be accomplished in his own lifetime. It seemed to Holgrave – as doubtless it has seemed to the hopeful of every century, since the epoch of Adam's grandchildren – that in this age, more than ever before, the moss-grown and rotten Past is to be torn down, and lifeless institutions to be thrust out of the way, and their dead corpses buried, and everything to begin anew. (2: 179)

This passage, too, reminds us of Hester's vision – not her concluding vision of reform in "Heaven's own time," but her earlier, more radical "freedom of speculation," which the Puritans would have "held to be a deadlier crime than that stigmatized by the scarlet letter" (1: 164). Thinking about the "dark question" involving the "whole race of womanhood," she recognizes that a revolution must occur: "As a first step, the whole system of society is to be torn down, and built up anew. Then, the very nature of the opposite sex, or its long hereditary habit, which has become like nature, is to be essentially modified, before woman can be allowed to assume what seems a fair and suitable position" (1: 165). In every novel except *The House of the Seven Gables*,

Hawthorne imagines a female character embodying the energy of reform or radicalism. Holgrave, a male Hester Prynne, carries that energy but ultimately doesn't use it. Holgrave must prove himself in different terms – within the domestic sphere.

Holgrave is also a mesmerist, or hypnotist, and his experience in this line enables Hawthorne to comment upon a popular nineteenth-century fad, especially as it pertains to male–female relationships. Hawthorne's depiction of mesmerism in *The House of the Seven Gables*, as well as in *The Blithedale Romance*, reminds many readers of the warning he issued to Sophia shortly before their marriage. Sophia had written him of her interest in mesmerism, and Hawthorne warned her to "take no part" in such "magnetic miracles":

> I am unwilling that a power should be exercised on thee, of which we know neither the origin nor consequence, and the phenomena of which seem rather calculated to bewilder us, than to teach us any truths about the present or future state of being. If I possessed such a power over thee, I should not dare to exercise it; nor can I consent to its being exercised by another. Supposing that this power arises from the transfusion of one spirit into another, it seems to me that the sacredness of an individual is violated by it; there would be an intrusion into thy holy of holies – and the intruder would not be thy husband! Canst thou think, without a shrinking of thy soul, of any human being coming into closer communion with thee than I may? – than either nature or my own sense of right would permit me? *I* cannot. And, dearest, thou must remember, too, that thou art now a part of me, and that by surrendering thyself to the influence of this magnetic lady, thou surrenderest more than thine own moral and spiritual being – allowing that the influence *is* a moral and spiritual one. And, sweetest, I really do not like the idea of being brought, through thy medium, into such an intimate relation with Mrs. Park! (15: 588)

We may cringe today at Hawthorne's condescending and paternalistic tone, but the passage resonates in several different registers. We recognize one of his favorite themes – the sanctity of individuality, which he typically figures as the human heart. In the forest scene in *The Scarlet Letter*, for example, Hester and Dimmesdale accuse Chillingworth of violating, "in cold blood, the sanctity of a human heart," while they congratulate themselves that they "never did so." The observation is followed immediately by Hester's famous declaration, "What we did had a consecration of its own" (1: 195). Hester's claim that adultery has a "consecration" of its own suggests that, unlike Chillingworth's efforts to penetrate Dimmesdale's interior, sexuality brings people into "closer communion" and thus echoes Hawthorne's advice to Sophia. There, too, mesmerism has a sexual aspect to it, but Hawthorne carefully distinguishes between good and bad sexual experience – consecrated and unconsecrated.

Hawthorne includes important mesmerical scenes in both *The House of the Seven Gables* and *The Blithedale Romance*, and in both instances he suggests a remarkable, if vexing congruence between the practice of mesmerism and the practice of romance writing. As Samuel Coale observes, as a "writer of what he called romances, he often saw himself as a kind of mesmerist/medium in which he used the very forces he himself morally opposed to describe and produce the techniques and strategies of his art."[12] The turning point in Holgrave's relationship with Phoebe in *The House of the Seven Gables* occurs in chapter 13, when Holgrave reads her a story he has written about Matthew Maule and Alice Pyncheon. Much as he had done in "Alice Doane's Appeal" and other early tales, Hawthorne emphasizes the power of male storytelling to captivate and seduce a female listener. Maule is one of Hawthorne's many mesmerical artists, a seductive artist who haunts and dominates the mind. He is "fabled" to possess a "strange power of getting into people's dreams, and regulating matters there according to his own fancy, pretty much like the stage-manager of a theatre" (2: 189), and he uses this power to control Alice. With sadistic relish he enjoys his power, humiliating her whenever possible by making her laugh or cry or dance wildly in public. His power is implicitly sexual, as "all the dignity of life was lost," and she "felt herself too much abased, and longed to change natures with some worm!" (2: 209). In addition to testing mesmeric power and associating it with his own art, Hawthorne also plays with nineteenth-century gender conventions. Alice trusts the "preservative force of womanhood" – a new gentility that idealized women into a sphere by themselves. Maule tests the power of an entrepreneurial manhood that views women as commodities to be marketed and displayed in public.

Holgrave's narrative varies the story Hawthorne told in "The Birth-mark" and "Rappaccini's Daughter": a story of woman's victimization and death at the hands of a male artist. In the context in which it appears, however, the narrative resembles "Alice Doane's Appeal" and the other early stories in which Hawthorne calculates his power to affect women readers. As noted, Hawthorne had expressed his fear of such mesmerical power being exercised on Sophia, because "there would be an intrusion into thy holy of holies – and the intruder would not be thy husband!" (15: 588). Here, as in Hawthorne's own case, that power is exercised on a woman by a man who would be her husband – a case of pre-marital "intrusion" into the "holy of holies." As Phoebe "leaned slightly towards him, and seemed almost to regulate her breath by his" (2: 211), Holgrave becomes aware that his power over her is "as dangerous, and perhaps as disastrous, as that which the carpenter of his legend had acquired and exercised over the ill-fated Alice" (2: 212). He can hardly keep himself from exercising this combined erotic and artistic power. "His glance, as he fastened it on the young girl, grew involuntarily more concentrated; in his attitude, there was the consciousness of power, investing his hardly mature figure with a dignity that did not belong to its physical manifestation" (2: 211).

In discovering himself as an artist, Holgrave stands revealed to himself as a lover–violator of the woman who has become the ideal "reader" of his story, that one heart and mind of a sympathy so perfect that she actually regulates her breathing by his. Although he recognizes that, if he indulged the one wish, he could act as Matthew Maule had acted toward Alice Pyncheon and "complete his mastery over Phoebe's yet free and virgin spirit" (2: 212), he resists temptation. The narrator approves, conceding to "the Daguerreotypist the rare and high quality of reverence for another's individuality" (2: 212). That reverence makes the rest of the story possible. Holgrave can reveal himself to be a (reformed, non-vengeful) Maule. Having proven himself a man who respects women, he can marry Phoebe. Love, not mesmeric power, will be the medium of their marriage.

Placing Holgrave in the position of sacrificing his radical ideas and force of character for a woman and a conventional relationship also means redefining him as a conventional man. As Chris Castiglia points out, the "transfer of power" to Holgrave that occurs at the end of the novel "symbolizes the triumph, in the decades just before Hawthorne wrote *The House of the Seven Gables*, of reform movements that targeted inner characteristics over the coercive mandates of external law."[13] Although Phoebe receives the most attention when critics focus on questions of gender in the novel, Hawthorne's construction and reconstruction of masculinity deserves equal attention.

At one male extreme is the effeminate Clifford Pyncheon, whose maleness is so attenuated that he is incapable of forming any productive ties with a woman. With his "full, tender lips and beautiful eyes" that "indicate not so much capacity of thought, as gentle and voluptuous emotion" (2: 32), Clifford is surely Hawthorne's most feminine male character. He has played the victim to the hyper-masculine Jaffrey Pyncheon, who framed him for a relative's murder and had him sent away to prison for years. "Insofar as modern homosexual identity gained public intelligibility as an inversion of Victorian gender roles," notes Castiglia, Clifford (and Hepzibah) "are arguably among American literature's first homosexual characters" ("Marvelous," 197).

At the other extreme, Jaffrey Pyncheon epitomizes nineteenth-century manhood on the make. His "sex, somehow or other, was entirely too prominent." While his "glowing benignity" might not be "absolutely unpleasant" to a woman, "with the width of a street or even an ordinary sized room interposed between," Jaffrey's presence "became quite too intense, when this dark, full-fed physiognomy (so roughly bearded, too, that no razor could ever make it smooth) sought to bring itself into actual contact with the object of its regards" (2: 118). Jaffrey embodies a rapacious, capitalist manhood – a "fat cat" who has political ambitions motivated largely by personal greed. Hawthorne represents him as especially offensive to women, thereby opposing the domestic sphere of the home to the world of work. His ancestor, "an autocrat in his own household, had worn out three wives," merely by the "remorseless weight and hardness of his character." Jaffrey has worn out his only wife in three or four years, after giving her a "death-blow" on their honeymoon – compelling her to "serve him with coffee, every morning, at his bedside, in token of fealty to her liege-lord and master" (2: 123).

Having proven himself to be a "good guy" when he refused to seduce Phoebe with his mesmerical power, Holgrave uses another of his arts – daguerreotypy – to exact revenge upon Jaffrey for his predatory exploitation of others. In the process Hawthorne takes revenge upon a particularly rapacious model of nineteenth-century manhood.

Developed in France by Louis Daguerre in the late 1830s, daguerreotypy became very popular in America in the 1840s and 1850s. The new technology plays an important role in *The House of the Seven Gables* and, like mesmerism, enables Hawthorne to test ideas about individual selfhood, as well as theories about art and narrative. Susan Williams notes, for example, that the "central viewing spaces in the text are framed windows": the display window of Hepzibah's shop, the arched window on the second floor of the house, the window of the train through which the fleeing Clifford and Hepzibah enjoy a dioramic view of the modern world they have avoided.[14] Painting, especially portrait painting, plays a role in the novel, too, but daguerreotypy obviously gives Hawthorne his most important frame of reference for the visual elements of the novel. Alan Trachtenberg, in fact, argues that Hawthorne recruited the daguerreotype "for a key role in the definition of 'Romance' that the narrative will unfold."[15] Whereas the mesmerist possessed a power to penetrate the self and disable individual agency, rendering the individual a puppet, daguerreotypy promised to produce a fixed image of the true self. Holgrave makes such a claim for the technology in *The House of the Seven Gables* when he assures Phoebe that, "while we give it credit only for depicting the merest surface, it actually brings out the secret character with a truth that no painter would ever venture upon" (2: 91).

Daguerreotypy stopped time, as the early versions of the technology required the subject to sit perfectly still for several minutes. When Hawthorne himself mimics daguerreotypy in *The House of the Seven Gables* in the remarkable

"Governor Pyncheon" chapter, he plays sadistically with the deadening effect of the new technology. The same process that stopped time and fixed an image of the self – thus promising to stabilize identity – imitated death, the ultimate state of changelessness. A dead body would be the ideal subject for the daguerreotypist, so in his extended description of the dead Jaffrey Pyncheon, as Cathy Davidson points out, Hawthorne/Holgrave indulges himself as a daguerreotypist might by forcing his subject to remain immovable while he as narrator moves around him, capturing every feature of his appearance.[16] "The Judge has not shifted his position for a long while," the narrator comments disingenuously. "He has not stirred hand or foot – nor withdrawn his eyes, so much as a hair's breadth, from their fixed gaze towards the corner of the room" (2: 268). This portrait of a dead capitalist indulges Hawthorne's desire to turn the tables on one of the most dastardly characters he had created. Jaffrey has framed Clifford for murder, and he announces his presence in the novel by attempting to force a kiss on Phoebe. When she recoils, Jaffrey ends up kissing the "empty air" (2: 118) – an outcome that Hawthorne, who made it happen, obviously applauds. The gesture and the embarrassing pose in which Jaffrey finds himself frozen – stopped in time much as he might have been in a daguerreotype – anticipate his death pose at the end of the novel.

Hawthorne situates Holgrave between the models of masculinity represented by Clifford and Jaffrey Pyncheon, as a man who might synthesize both extremes into a masculinity that incorporates the feminine. Holgrave comes from the world of work and entrepreneurial, speculative manhood, but he is domesticated over the course of the novel so that he can occupy a comfortable place in the home. His refusal to act on the threat to Phoebe that his identity as a Maule seems to require breaks a cycle of exploitation and violence that had started many years before and thus makes possible an alternative ending to a narrative that could have been determined by a historical fatalism of repetition. Holgrave's refusal to seduce Phoebe through art anticipates Coverdale and Kenyon, who surrender even more power to women. Both *The Blithedale Romance* and *The Marble Faun*, in fact, feature a female character who would not only read a story like Holgrave's, but probably write one of her own.

The ending of each of Hawthorne's novels has provoked controversy. Having Hester return to Boston and resume the scarlet letter seems to betray her radical potential, and the ending that Holgrave makes in *The House of the Seven Gables* disappoints readers for the same reason. Holgrave's marriage to Phoebe and revelation that he is a Maule make the ending conventional – the expected resolution of class and character conflict through marriage. Holgrave, however, has been bought off – or chosen to be. As Lang points out, the money that Phoebe inherits and Holgrave acquires through marriage "reifies the divide between rich and poor and ensures its continuance" (*Syntax*, 32). Or as Gillian Brown argues, "the romance spun out in this commercial success story allays nervousness about the risks of commerce with a fairy-tale ending of restored wealth and health; the trials of the market are so thoroughly overcome that the reality of free enterprise democracy seems to disappear in the closing scene of retirement to an inherited country estate."[17] The Maules and Pyncheons may have resolved their differences, which are rooted in class and a longstanding property dispute, but the Pyncheon estate remains intact. Phoebe presumably becomes Phoebe Maule, but it would seem more appropriate for Holgrave to change his name to Pyncheon. The radical Holgrave, who seemed determined to turn society upside down and level distinctions, turns out to be gold-digger who marries for money.

The Blithedale Romance

The Blithedale Romance was obviously based on Hawthorne's experiences at Brook Farm, even if the main plot – the shifting relations among the four principal characters (Coverdale, Zenobia, Hollingsworth, and Priscilla) – was not. Writing coyly in the Preface, Hawthorne acknowledged that "many readers will probably suspect a faint and not very faithful shadowing of Brook Farm, in Roxbury," and he admitted that he did not "wish to deny, that he had this Community in his mind." But he claimed that his "whole treatment of the affair" of Brook Farm was "altogether incidental to the main purpose of the Romance."[18]

In composing every one of his novels, Hawthorne resorted to a nineteenth-century version of "cut-and-paste," interpolating notebook passages into the text, largely to help him with characters and setting. *The Blithedale Romance* includes many passages from Hawthorne's notebooks, most but not all from the time he lived at Brook Farm. An "elderly ragamuffin, in a dingy and battered hat" (8: 496), whom he had seen in a Boston saloon, becomes Old Moodie, while the saloon itself provides the setting for chapter 21 of the novel ("An Old Acquaintance"). A young seamstress from Boston, who lived briefly at Brook Farm, forms the basis of Priscilla's character (8: 209–10). Coverdale's hermitage – the tree house to which he retreats several times in *Blithedale* in order to observe others without being seen – derives from a description Hawthorne recorded at Cow Island near Brook Farm on September 26, 1841, and also includes the grapevines and luscious grapes that Coverdale makes such a point of emphasizing (8: 197–98). The scene of masquerade in chapter 24 of *Blithedale* is transcribed from a September 28, 1841, entry that includes a fascinating detail that Hawthorne excludes from the novel – a visit to Brook Farm by Ralph Waldo Emerson and Margaret Fuller (8: 201–03). And as already noted, Hawthorne worked up his lengthy description of retrieving the drowned body of Martha Hunt into chapter 27 ("Midnight") of the novel, in which Coverdale and others search for Zenobia's body, even though that event occurred in Concord several years after he left Brook Farm.

As Hawthorne's only extended first-person narrative, *The Blithedale Romance* has intrigued readers and critics for the way it foregrounds questions of narrative reliability. As an artist, a "Minor Poet, beginning life with strenuous aspirations, which die out with his youthful fervor" (3: 2–3), Miles Coverdale hopes to "produce something that shall really deserve to be called poetry – true, strong, natural, and sweet" (3: 14), but his artistic prowess hardly matters as the narrative unfolds. Instead of being a creator, he spends most of the novel passively watching a drama involving other characters. He moves in and out of the triangle these other characters form, testing the possibility of a personal relationship with each of them, but he remains a bachelor who finally seems little interested in relationships.

Hawthorne, on the other hand, does seem interested in experimenting with different configurations of character relations and in exploring the possibility of several different combinations. Much more than *The Scarlet Letter*, in which Hester could imagine a reordering of male–female relationships, *The Blithedale Romance* opens the possibility of same-sex, as well as opposite-sex, attraction. The "footing, on which we all associated at Blithedale," Coverdale notes, "was widely different from that of conventional society." Since he had just published a novel, *The House of the Seven Gables*, which paid homage to conventional society, at least in its relationships, Hawthorne seemed to be marking out a more radical path in *Blithedale* by recognizing, as Robert Martin notes, a "plurality of desires."[19] "While inclining us to the soft affections of the Golden Age," Coverdale observes, "it seemed to authorize any individual, of either sex, to fall in love with any other, regardless of what would elsewhere be judged suitable and prudent" (3: 72).

Homosexuality did not exist as a term when Hawthorne wrote *The Blithedale Romance* in 1852. Love and sexual relationships between men obviously did exist. Several chapters after this utopian declaration of independence, Hawthorne challenges Coverdale to try out the least conventional of the relationships he had imagined, when Hollingsworth asks him to be his "friend of friends forever" and to join him in his philanthropical project of criminal rehabilitation (3: 135). "Take it up with me!" Hollingsworth urges. "Be my brother in it!" "Strike hands with me; and from this moment, you shall never again feel the languor and vague wretchedness of an indolent or half-occupied man!" Instead, Hollingsworth promises, Coverdale shall enjoy "everything that a manly and generous nature should desire!" Hollingsworth's eyes fill with tears at this moment, and he reaches out his hands to Coverdale, murmuring, "there is not the man in this wide world whom I can love as I could you. Do not foresake me!" (3: 133). Coverdale interrupts the narrative momentum at this point, backing us (and himself) out of the scene in its own present time to recall it from the distance of the current present moment:

> As I look back upon this scene, through the coldness and dimness of so many years, there is still a sensation as if Hollingsworth had caught hold of my heart, and were pulling it towards him with an almost irresistible force. It is a mystery to me, how I withstood it. But in truth, I saw in his scheme of philanthropy nothing but what was odious. A loathsomeness that was to be forever in my daily work! A great, black ugliness of sin, which he proposed to collect out of a thousand human hearts, and that we should spend our lives in an experiment of transmuting into virtue! Had I but touched his extended hand, Hollingsworth's magnetism would perhaps have penetrated me with his own conception of all these matters. But I stood aloof.   (3: 134)

This is one of the passages scholars cite when they consider *The Blithedale Romance* to register Hawthorne's response to the friendship he had enjoyed with Herman Melville. Critics interested in exploring Melville's representation of homosocial or homosexual relationships cite the suggestive language found in several of Melville's letters to Hawthorne, his review of *Mosses from an Old Manse*, the apparent reference to loving Hawthorne in the poem "Monody," and the depiction of Hawthorne in the character of Vine in *Clarel*. The review, with its provocative image of Hawthorne's "soft ravishments" spinning Melville "around in a web of dreams," of Hawthorne dropping "germinous seeds" into Melville's soul and then shooting his "strong New-England roots" into the "hot soil" of Melville's "Southern soul," has warranted many analyses.[20] Hollingsworth's command to "strike hands," for example, echoes Captain Ahab's request that the men "splice hands" with him in his quest to kill Moby Dick more than it reminds us of Ishmael's Spouter Inn marriage to Queequeg or the scene in which he squeezes spermaceti with other members of the *Pequod*'s crew.[21] The earlier scene in which Hollingsworth attends the sick Coverdale, who has been confined to his bed, does recall the scene at the Spouter Inn, as Coverdale approvingly notes Hollingsworth's "more than brotherly attendance" (3: 41).

Edwin Haviland Miller claims that the Coverdale–Hollingsworth relationship is at the "heart" of the novel. He views Coverdale as a "self-portrait of

Hawthorne's seeming weaknesses and effeminacy as artist and chilled, detached observer," while Hollingsworth "embodies Melville's aggression and need of a 'brother.'"[22] Monica Mueller argues more reductively that the scene in which Hollingsworth propositions Coverdale can be figured as an attempted "homosexual rape." "Afraid of being penetrated by Hollingsworth's phallic, rigid philanthropic idea," Coverdale "rebuffs his friend," reacting so violently against the "object" position in which this attempted rape places him that he determines to prove his manhood by differentiating himself from women.[23] Without assuming that a scene like this one actually occurred between Hawthorne and Melville, it does seem likely that Melville looms in the background of this scene. It also seems likely that *Moby-Dick*, the marriage between Ishmael and Queequeg and its scene of ecstatic sperm- and hand-squeezing between men, also figures in Hawthorne's imagination.

Coverdale's response to Hollingsworth suggests spontaneous homophobia. Coverdale displaces his revulsion from Hollingsworth to the philanthropical project, but his language – "odious," "loathsomeness," "black ugliness of sin" – is so obviously excessive when applied to the project that we infer, anachronistically, a case of homosexual panic. Coverdale's nineteenth-century version of homophobia also marks his response to Westervelt. Although he considers Westervelt "as handsome a man as ever I beheld" (3: 91), he seems to catch himself immediately. Westervelt's "style of beauty" does not "commend itself" to his taste; there is an "indecorum" in his face, and there is in his eyes the "naked exposure of something that ought not to be left prominent" (3: 91–92). "I hated him," Coverdale concludes (3: 92).

Not surprisingly, Coverdale leaves Blithedale for a vacation very shortly after this encounter with Hollingsworth. He will return, although not for long, but the possibility of a friendship with Hollingsworth becomes increasingly remote. In fact, the plurality of relational possibilities seems foreclosed upon, and insofar as the rest of Coverdale's narrative engages the question of relationship, it limits its concern to the potential pairings of male and female characters.

Although Coverdale never convinces us that he is seriously interested in giving up his bachelorhood, he does flirt with the thought of relationships with both Zenobia and Priscilla. The issue is largely symbolic, as each female character highlights different potentials and limitations in Coverdale's manhood. Nina Baym argues that "Coverdale's intention of tapping the soul's reservoir of energy, of contacting its passionate, creative, active principle requires a representation in the romance of that underlying principle."[24] Zenobia becomes a symbol of that principle and subjects Coverdale to a series of challenging experiences. She supervises his education, limited though it finally is, in the nature of women and the complexities of art. As both object and subject, Zenobia resists what Mary Suzanne Schriber calls the "limitations of conventions, the limitations Coverdale continually attempts to force upon her in order to bring her within the sphere of his understanding."[25] Hawthorne termed her a "high-spirited Woman, bruising herself against the narrow limitations of her sex" (3: 2) – simultaneously identifying her creative power and foreshadowing her fate.

Although Zenobia certainly speaks some powerful lines in the novel, she figures for Coverdale much more as an object than as a subject. Associated with openness, fluidity, and extraordinary energy, she is "all alive, to her finger-tips" (3: 16) and has "free, careless, generous modes of expression" that cause Coverdale to imagine her naked – in "Eve's earliest garment" (3: 17). Far from being a stereotype, Zenobia resists containment by type or by language. Her presence always implies more than Coverdale can denote. As a character who encourages images in his mind which, "though pure, are hardly felt to be quite decorous, when born of a thought that passes between man and woman" (3: 17), she threatens his narrative control. Her power as an object is indicated by the defensive strategies Coverdale brings to bear upon her. He would prefer to repress his "naked" thoughts of her altogether. She challenges his ability to "clothe" his thoughts in language, and she certainly offers him an opportunity to put his own relationship to women on a new footing. Historically and culturally considered, she represents everything that has been "refined away out of the feminine system" (3: 17). Despite the decorously objectified form in which Coverdale tries to imagine her, throughout the novel Zenobia threatens to break out of any mold in which his imagination tries to confine her.

The most important example occurs in the scene at Eliot's pulpit, when Zenobia stands and speaks in her role as powerful feminist reformer. When Coverdale smiles at her vow to use her voice "in behalf of woman's wider liberty," she flashes a look with "anger in her eyes," and lectures him about the plight of women: "It is my belief – yes, and my prophecy, should I die before it happens that, when my sex shall achieve its rights, there will be ten eloquent women, where there is now one eloquent man" (3: 120). Zenobia's "prophecy" is considerably stronger than Hester Prynne's appeal to Heaven's own time, and her indictment of Coverdale is the most direct of the many challenges she poses to his imagination and thought.

Mesmerism plays a more central role in *The Blithedale Romance* than in *The House of the Seven Gables*, but in this novel too it offers Hawthorne a medium for exploring issues of control in male–female relationships. Indeed, Coale says that it "permeates and upends the romance" as if "it were the only reality, however morally questionable and downright demonic" (*Mesmerism*, 119). Most intriguingly, Coale argues that Hawthorne's use of mesmerism in

The Blithedale Romance enables him to explore the psychology of slavery – the "psychological domination of master over slave and the willing submission of slave to master" (113). Much as he had done in *The House of the Seven Gables*, when Holgrave reads Phoebe his story of Alice Pyncheon, Hawthorne includes an embedded or framed story in *The Blithedale Romance* – reversing the gender positions by having Zenobia recount the legend of the Veiled Lady for Coverdale's benefit and instruction. In this case, too, the tale-within-the-tale rehearses the main themes of the romance in miniaturized form. Zenobia stages her narration by using Priscilla as a prop, for of course the story of the Veiled Lady is Priscilla's story, and the difference between character and prop dissolves at the climax, when Zenobia throws a gauzy veil over Priscilla's head. Coverdale, however, misses the point, ignoring the lesson of Theodore's failure to kiss the Veiled Lady before he sees her face and so seemingly disqualifying himself for a relationship with either of the sisters.

Furthermore, when Coverdale attends the mesmerism exhibition at the Lyceum, he comes close to acting out Theodore's experience with the Veiled Lady, as if matching himself to the character of Zenobia's tale. He views the mesmerist as an artist for whom human character is "but soft wax in his hands." Earlier he had remarked upon Priscilla's "pleasant weakness" (3: 74) and had called her "impressible as wax" (3: 78), so his language identifies him with the mesmerist. Indeed, Hawthorne makes clear, the ideal relationship for Coverdale would be a mesmerical one – a relationship in which a woman would be under his imaginative control. Most important, he stresses the sexual or seductive power that the mesmerist enjoys over his young female subject – his power to turn her passion for a lover, with his kiss "still burning on her lips," into "icy indifference" (3: 198). Hawthorne had expressed the fear that the mesmerist might violate Sophia's "holy of holies" and had vowed not to use such power. Coverdale would go a step further, using mesmerical attraction to freeze rather than inflame passion. That is, Coverdale does not really seek a physical relationship with a woman; he seeks an imaginative one. His speculations are consistent with the sort of fantastical relationship he covets in his memories of Priscilla. Even at the end of the novel, she remains a Veiled Lady. Hollingsworth, after all, releases her from her bondage to Westervelt. Hollingsworth, not Coverdale, steps through the frame of the work of art to dissolve the threat it poses to her. Coverdale, in contrast, has been effectively mesmerized by Westervelt's exhibition and so rendered powerless to help Priscilla. In effect, Hawthorne suggests, Coverdale is so captivated by his fantasies of women that he cannot apprehend the real thing.

Many critics have complained about Coverdale's breathless declaration of love for Priscilla in the last sentence of the novel, as well as about Zenobia's ignominious death, and there is much to be said for the judgment that Hawthorne simply could not tolerate such a powerful character. A few critics have even mounted a case against Coverdale as Zenobia's murderer. Louise DeSalvo, for example, claims that, "within the context of the novel, that Zenobia is murdered is as likely a conclusion as that she committed suicide, and given the content of Coverdale's consciousness, he would be the likely suspect."[26] Since Coverdale has persistently tried to objectify Zenobia, it seems perversely appropriate that she satisfy his desire by turning up as a corpse. Ironically, as both object and subject, as image and voice, she has a dynamic life after death. The test of her residual power is her effect on Coverdale's imagination and on his narrative.

In death, her body locked in one position by rigor mortis, she assumes a posture of "terrible inflexibility," a "marble image of a death-agony" (3: 235). But even in this condition, Zenobia retains considerable vitality for Coverdale's imagination. Although limited to this single attitude, she at least assumes an energetic one – a posture of rebellion, "as if she struggled against Providence in never-ending hostility," her hands "clenched in immitigable defiance" (3: 235). Indeed, Zenobia's hostile appearance has burned itself indelibly into Coverdale's imagination. His earlier desire to subject her to the "cold decorum" of marble has had a paradoxical effect, and even his impulse to close his eyes in her presence will avail him little. His imagination is finally impotent to regulate, much less contain, Zenobia's presence. While Coverdale ends his narrative with a declaration of love for Priscilla, he admits that Zenobia's memory haunts him more. "For more than twelve long years I have borne it in my memory," he admits, "and could now reproduce it as freshly as if it were still before my eyes" (3: 235).

The Marble Faun

In his 1879 book on Hawthorne for the English Men of Letters series, Henry James commented that *The Marble Faun* (1860) forms "part of the intellectual equipment of the Anglo-Saxon visitor to Rome, and is read by every English-speaking traveller who arrives there, who has been there, or who expects to go."[27] The views of nineteenth-century readers were hardly unanimous, some reviewers complaining that Hawthorne wrote a guide book when he meant to write a novel, and contemporary readers generally prefer Hawthorne's earlier novels to his last one. In some key respects, the novel is not that different, especially from *The Blithedale Romance*. Hawthorne recycles the characters and plot he had used in *Blithedale*, hanging the story on a character foursome whose allegiances and perhaps love for one another shift from object to object over the course of the narrative – producing a similar, though not identical, romantic resolution. The four characters bear obvious resemblances to their counterparts in *The Blithedale Romance*. Miriam Schaefer, like Zenobia, derives from the Dark Lady tradition of American romance, but she exceeds the confines of that stereotype, especially in her role as an artist – the most successful woman artist in Hawthorne's fiction. Like Priscilla, Hilda, the young American woman, is a type of Pale Maiden – a weaker character than Miriam, but a person with religious convictions that make her a rigid moralist. The sculptor, Kenyon, seems to be a more successful artist than Miles Coverdale, and like the earlier character he finds himself attracted for very different reasons to both Miriam and Hilda. The faun-like Donatello, Miriam's friend and eventual lover, resembles Hollingsworth somewhat, at least in representing a type of natural manhood. Unlike the dour, super-serious Hollingsworth, Donatello is boyish, impulsive, and fun-loving.

Despite Kenyon's declaration of love for the Pale Maiden, Hilda, at the end of the novel, Miriam dominates much of the narrative and consistently challenges Kenyon's imagination just as Zenobia had challenged Coverdale's. In both *The Blithedale Romance* and *The Marble Faun*, in fact, Hawthorne empowers his strong female characters to such an extent that it is easy to conclude that he finds them much more attractive and compelling than the weaker women who seem finally to capture the protagonist's heart. The ending of each novel seems fake and forced, partly because Coverdale and Kenyon end up with the "wrong" woman. On the other hand, these forced endings may suggest that Hawthorne's main interest is not really in a marriage plot – that a declaration of love or impending marriage represents a concession to popular tastes and expectations. Perhaps we should focus our attention on the middle of each narrative and on Hawthorne's experimentation with various character relationships.

Nina Baym argues that Miriam's "passion, creativity, and spontaneity" must be "accepted if man is to do her justice and grow to his own fullest expression."[28] At the same time, Miriam possesses a strength of character and will, a desire to define and create herself, at least equal to Zenobia's or Hester Prynne's. She has, and expresses, a strength of her own that does not depend on fulfillment in relationship. As an artist within the work of art, she exercises more artistic freedom than Hester Prynne, and given the power she wields over Kenyon's imagination – a power to direct his actions and inspire him temporarily to sculpt – she seems more powerful than even Zenobia. Most important, Miriam is a very successful artist – a feminist artist. Her most striking paintings (of Jael, Judith, and Salome) represent murderous women who seek vengeance against men. She calls such images "ugly phantoms that stole out of my mind; not things that I created, but things that haunt me" (4: 45), thus linking herself directly to Hawthorne's most creative characters and to Hawthorne himself. Miriam even makes her paintings come true in the world of the novel. She gains revenge upon the model who persecutes her by convincing Donatello to kill him.

With more freedom than Hester or Zenobia, Miriam is able to create an art object that expresses herself – fulfilling the ideal Hawthorne had established for the most creative women, of coming before the world "stark naked" (see chapter 2). The portrait represents a

> beautiful woman, such as one sees only two or three, if even so many, in all a lifetime; so beautiful, that she seemed to get into your consciousness and memory, and could never afterwards be shut out, but haunted your dreams, for pleasure or for pain; holding your inner realm as a conquered territory, though without deigning to make herself at home there. (4: 47–48)

Hawthorne's narrator compares her to Rachel, but also to Judith, "when she vanquished Holofernes with her beauty" (4: 48) – thus eliding the difference between Miriam's vengeful paintings and her self-portrait. Unlike Zenobia, who appeared to give up the fight for women and for her rightful place in society, Miriam will revenge herself upon those who oppress her.

As an artist Hilda stands in sharp contrast to Miriam. Essentially a copyist, she idealizes her subjects, abstracting them into their "spirit and essence" (4: 58). Seeing the world through Hilda's art is like "looking at humanity with angel's eyes" (4: 55). Whereas Miriam paints women avenging themselves upon men, Hilda copies the works of male painters, the Old Masters. Hilda seems a lot like Phoebe Pyncheon in *The House of the Seven Gables* in the purifying power she exercises. Within the realm of art she performs a conventional nineteenth-century domestic role – an Angel of the Studio rather than an Angel of the House.

Hawthorne had little first-hand experience with sculpture before he visited Italy, but the studios and museums he visited there quickly captured his interest, and he based *The Marble Faun* on a statue (Praxiteles' *Faun*) he saw at the Capitoline Museum in Rome.[29] In earlier works he had emphasized sculpture's power to freeze and purify bodies, as in Coverdale's reference in *The Blithedale Romance* to the "cold decorum of the marble" (3: 41). Coverdale uses that figure to contain his thoughts of Zenobia, whom he has earlier imagined in "Eve's earliest garment" (3: 17) and whose "flesh-warmth" and "full bust" cause him to close his eyes, "as if it were not quite the privilege of modesty to gaze at her" (3: 41). Hawthorne praised the American sculptor Hiram Powers's statue

California, which he found "as naked as Venus," precisely because she was "not an actual woman, capable of exciting passion, but evidently a little out of the category of human nature" (14: 281). In *The Marble Faun* Hawthorne asserts that marble assumes a "sacred character," and "no man should dare to touch it unless he feels within himself a certain consecration and a priesthood" (4: 136). When Kenyon criticizes the Dying Gladiator (a sculpture that occupies the same room in the Capitoline Museum as the Marble Faun), Miriam claims that he considers sculpture a "fossilizing process" (4: 16). "You turn feverish men," she later accuses him, "into cool, quiet marble" (4: 119). These passages suggest a conflict in Hawthorne's attitude toward nudity in sculpture.

Sculpture vexed Hawthorne as much as it captivated him, because it broke down the distance – figured as a "neutral territory" – between the artist and his material and, in turn, between the viewer and the work of art. Hawthorne felt scandalized, or at least pretended to be, when he described his visit to Hiram Powers's studio in Florence in 1858. A native Vermonter who had also worked for a number of years in Cincinnati, Ohio, Powers was best-known for his sculpture *The Greek Slave*, which toured the United States to great acclaim in 1847–48, provoking some controversy because of its nudity and obvious allusion to slavery. When Hawthorne visited him, Powers was working on a sculpture of George Washington:

> Powers took us into the farthest room, I believe, of his very extensive studio, and showed us a statue of Washington that has much dignity and stateliness; he expressed, however, great contempt for the coat and breeches, and masonic emblems, in which he had been required to drape the figure. What the devil would the man do with Washington, the most decorous and respectable personage that ever went ceremoniously through the realities of life! Did anybody ever see Washington naked! It is inconceivable. He had no nakedness, but, I imagine, was born with his clothes on and his hair powdered, and made a stately bow on his first appearance in the world. His costume, at all events, was a part of his character, and must be dealt with by whatever sculptor undertakes to represent him. I wonder that so very sensible a man as Powers should not see the necessity of accepting drapery; and the very drapery of the day, if he will keep his art alive. It is his business to idealize the tailor's actual work. But he seems to be especially fond of nudity, none of his ideal statues – so far as I know them – having so much as a rag of clothes.   (14: 281)

Hawthorne wants Washington to be clothed – with no hint of an underlying nakedness. Preferring the draped Washington and refusing so pointedly to imagine him naked, especially in the context of Hiram Powers's desire to take off Washington's clothes, serves Hawthorne as the proverbial pink elephant – making male nakedness displayed to other men the very thing he can't help but imagine. As Hawthorne himself wondered, "What the devil would the man do with Washington?"

Attitudes toward sculpted nudity changed during the eighteenth and nineteenth centuries, as preferences for male nudes gave way before preferences for nude women, and that change in taste occurred at the same time that proscriptions against homoerotic behavior between men and the tendency to derive male subjectivity and male identity from sexual behavior increased. The result was a reorientation of the male gaze and its significance, at least when the gaze figures relationships between men and sculpted male bodies. Joy Kasson has brilliantly examined Powers's *Greek Slave* within a framework of "Narratives of the Female Body," but she and other critics assume that the sculptural gaze is male and takes women as its object. *The Marble Faun*, however, offers a narrative of the male body that arises through the power of male-to-male gazing.[30] That is, representing men viewing statues of naked men enables Hawthorne to explore male-to-male relationships. What the devil would a man do with the sculpted body of another man?

More than Victorian prudishness before the "apotheosis of nudity" he discovered in Italy (14: 111), Hawthorne's anxiety before Powers's Washington has its origins in the way he thinks about sculpture – in his preference for clay over marble. A sculptor has very little to do with "actually chiseling the marble," he comments in *The Marble Faun* (4: 115). The "exquisitely designed shape of clay," in fact, is "more interesting than even the final marble, as being the intimate production of the sculptor himself, moulded throughout with his loving hands, and nearest to his imagination and heart" (4: 114). Miriam comments that she will not touch clay because it is "earthy and human" (4: 116), and sculpture fascinates and frightens Hawthorne because it offers such a sensual, hands-on experience of mortal embodiment. The model's death in *The Marble Faun* represents a reversal of this creative process – the disintegration of a male body into a mass or "heap" of raw material – and Hawthorne felt haunted by this possibility and image, an ultimate nakedness and abjectness that he felt reluctant to touch. Were you not afraid to touch your clay model of Cleopatra, Miriam asks Kenyon during her visit to his studio, "as she grew more and more towards hot life, beneath your hand?" (4: 127).

The specter that Powers's Washington raises for Hawthorne involves just this sort of "intimate production" – the play of the sculptor's hands over a man's rather than a woman's naked body. The result is another nineteenth-century example of homosexual panic. As Kenyon explains, when Miriam accuses him of taking Donatello away from her, "I am a man, and, between man and man, there is always an insuperable gulf. They can never quite grasp each other's hands; and therefore man never derives any intimate help, any heart-sustenance, from his brother man" (4: 285). Hawthorne's encounter with Powers's sculpture of Washington, as well as his representation of sculptured masculinity in *The Marble Faun*, raises critical questions about male-to-male relationships and how such relationships could be embodied and translated into narrative in nineteenth-century literature. Using sculpture puts him at one remove from actual men, although sculpted images sometimes come to life.

Even though readers sometimes complain that Hawthorne devotes too much attention to the Roman setting, as if he were writing a guidebook, I think he does a fascinating job of working sculpture and conflicts about sculpture into the novel. Each of the four main characters is associated with sculpture at some point in the book, and Hawthorne uses sculpture as a sounding board to test his characters' feelings for and attitudes toward one another. Miriam acknowledges the transgressive, erotic power of art, for example, even as she echoes Hawthorne's notebook commentary on nudity in sculpture. "Now-a-days people are as good as born in their clothes," she says, "and there is practically not a nude human being in existence. An artist, therefore, – as you must candidly confess, – cannot sculpture nudity with a pure heart, if only because he is compelled to steal guilty glimpses at hired models. The marble inevitably loses its chastity under such circumstances" (4: 123). A variation on the erotic–aesthetic concern for the sculptor's "hot" touch, this anxiety involves a failure of representation – a fear that the "cold decorum of marble" cannot distract the sculptor's attention from the "real thing" before his gaze. In both cases, Hawthorne's anxiety expresses the tendency of bodies to displace their representations. Kenyon's prized possession, after all, is a sculpted replica of Hilda's "small, beautifully shaped hand," but even this decorous surrogate, which Kenyon dares not kiss (4: 122), won't reside inertly within the cold decorum of the marble. "Touching those lovely fingers – had the jealous sculptor allowed you to touch – you could hardly believe that a virgin warmth would not steal from them into your heart" (4: 120).

In confusing the boundaries between art and life, statues and men, in his depiction of the Marble Faun, Hawthorne plays dangerously with possibilities he had foreclosed in his response to Powers's Washington. Fondling clay is one thing; fondling clay that embodies a man is another. Miriam suggests that the distinction between real and marble men cannot so easily be maintained, when she notes the resemblance between Donatello and the *Faun* of Praxiteles. She judges that the "portraiture is perfect in character, sentiment, and feature. If it were a picture, the resemblance might be half-illusive and imaginary; but here, in this Pentelic marble, it is a substantial fact, and may be tested by absolute touch and measurement" (4: 7). Hawthorne goes on in his own voice – the voice of his notebook directly transcribed into the novel – to affirm that Donatello "might have figured perfectly as the marble Faun, miraculously softened into flesh and blood" (4: 8). The Faun is the "marble image of a young man, leaning his right arm on the trunk or stump of a tree," he observes;

> one hand hangs carelessly by his side; in the other he holds the fragment of a pipe, or some such sylvan instrument of music. His only garment – a lion's skin, with the claw upon his shoulder – falls half-way down his back, leaving the limbs and entire front of the figure nude. The form, thus displayed, is marvellously graceful, but has a fuller and more rounded outline, more flesh, and less of heroic muscle, than the old sculptors were wont to assign to their types of masculine beauty. The character of the face corresponds with the figure; it is most agreeable in outline and feature, but rounded, and somewhat voluptuously developed, especially about the throat and chin; the nose is almost straight, but very slightly curves inward, thereby acquiring an indescribable charm of geniality and humour. The mouth, with its full, yet delicate lips, seems so nearly to smile outright, that it calls forth a responsive smile. The whole statue – unlike anything else that ever was wrought in that severe material of marble – conveys the idea of an amiable and sensual creature, easy, mirthful, apt for jollity, yet not incapable of being touched by pathos. It is impossible to gaze long at this stone image without conceiving a kindly sentiment towards it, as if its substance were warm to the touch, and imbued with actual life. It comes very close to some of our pleasantest sympathies.   (4: 8–9)

Unlike the desire that Hawthorne carefully checks as he contemplates Powers's statue of Washington, the play of male desire across the surface of the Marble Faun carries an animating, eroticizing power and, surprisingly for an author who preferred "neutral territories," raises the prospect of a barely mediated tactile experience – the possibility of "absolute touch." The act of gazing activates a "kindly sentiment" that renders the statue "warm to the touch"; the man of marble becomes "imbued with actual life" through the power of male desire.

Hawthorne had certainly explored the possibility in *The Blithedale Romance* of an intimate friendship between men and had used erotic language in doing so. The relationship between Coverdale and Hollingsworth in the earlier book has its counterpart in *The Marble Faun* in the relationship between Kenyon and Donatello. In this case, Hawthorne uses sculpture to mediate that relationship. The Marble Faun embodies coarseness and physicality, a male body unrestrained by clothing or manner and possessing a "capacity for strong and warm attachment" (4: 9). Hawthorne marvels at the sculptor's "rare artistic skill" and "delicate taste" – the way he managed the obvious tension between desire and representation, letting loose his imagination to dream "a Faun in this guise" but then succeeding in "imprisoning the sportive and frisky thing, in marble." "Neither man nor animal, and yet no monster," Hawthorne concludes, "but a being in whom both races meet, on friendly ground" (4: 10). Working hard to portray the Faun as another "neutral territory," Hawthorne's best effort produces a male body that reflects an uneasy truce between desire and its expression – a prison-house of desire, sportive and frisky, that threatens to burst forth a monster.

The Faun might be considered a neutral territory in another respect as well. For in displaying a "graceful" and "more rounded outline," and less "heroic muscle" than the classical model of masculine beauty would predict, the Praxiteles *Faun* seems to occupy a place somewhere between conventional genders. Abigail Solomon-Godeau explicitly links the Praxiteles *Faun* to a tradition of representing ephebic (young, unformed) manhood, and she illustrates the point by juxtaposing the *Faun* and the Farnese *Hercules*, which excessively embodies an opposite tradition – of virile, dominating, masculinity.[31] Hawthorne understood the implications of these different male body types, because he himself had employed them in contrasting Owen Warland and Robert Danforth in "The Artist of the Beautiful" and Coverdale and Hollingsworth in *The Blithedale Romance*. He seems initially more comfortable with the ephebic ideal in *The Marble Faun*, naturalizing it in the observation that the Faun represents a "poet's reminiscence of a period when man's affinity with Nature was more strict, and his fellowship with every living thing more intimate and dear" (4: 11). The Faun is transgendered enough that, when Hawthorne first saw the statue and recorded his response in his notebook, he imagined himself incarnating the Faun's fascinating combination of characteristics "in the person of a young lady" (14: 179). Transcribing such a transgendered male body into narrative and bringing it to life raises significant questions about "natural" manhood precisely where the male body and the male gaze intersect. What is natural, Hawthorne seems to say, depends upon who is doing the looking and what sort of desire he brings to the process. Gender, not just beauty, is in the eye of the beholder.

Nancy Bentley and Kristie Hamilton have analyzed Hawthorne's exploration of primitivism and its connection to American racial issues in the 1860s. Bentley shows how Donatello can be considered a type of African American character, while Hamilton examines his Native American Indian characteristics.[32] I would like to build upon their insights by examining Hawthorne's interest in

Donatello's "naturalism" – what it means for him to reminisce about a period and a condition in which "man's affinity with nature was more strict." It is hard to imagine a man less constructed – less like Powers's Washington – than Donatello as he first appears. In contrast to Washington, Donatello seems a naked and natural man. As Kenyon puts it, "Nature needed, and still needs, this beautiful creature, standing betwixt man and animal, sympathizing with each, comprehending the speech of either race, and interpreting the whole existence of one to the other" (4: 13). Or, in Miriam's terms: "how happy, how genial, how satisfactory would be his life, enjoying the warm, sensuous, earthy side of nature; revelling in the merriment of woods and streams; living as our four-footed kindred do – as mankind did in its innocent childhood, before sin, sorrow, or morality itself had ever been thought of!" (4: 13). Aside from the obvious Edenic reference in his story of a Fortunate Fall, both statements suggest more particular references, especially in the context of sculpture. "So full of animal life," "so physically well-developed," "exacting no strict obedience to conventional rules" (4: 77), Donatello is no Marble Faun, even though Hawthorne explicitly compares him to the Praxiteles sculpture. His "natural" condition suggests a man still in the clay, so to speak, who possesses various transgressive powers. Hawthorne plays coy, for example, in his description of Donatello's ears and "caudal appendage." The "mute mystery" that Praxiteles has "diffused" throughout his work makes determining the precise species of the Faun problematical.

Having posited Donatello's naturalness, Hawthorne emphasizes how Donatello's later experience, especially his murder of Miriam's model in chapter 18, reconstructs him as a man who represses natural pleasure. Shortly after the murder, for example, Kenyon notices Donatello's "newly acquired power of dealing with his own emotions, and, after a struggle more or less fierce, thrusting them down into the prison-cells where he usually kept them confined" (4: 250). At the moment of transformation, Donatello's body "seemed to have dilated" and his eyes blaze with "fierce energy"; he is "kindled" into a man whose murderous rage toward another man replaces the natural passion we have seen (4: 172). In killing the model, however, Donatello trades positions with him. He ceases to resemble the Praxiteles *Faun* because he now seems more human. The model becomes "stone dead," a "dark mass," or "heap, with little or nothing human in its appearance" (4: 173). When Miriam sees him laid out in the Capuchin Church, he is a "form of clay" (4: 192). Simultaneously, Hawthorne imagines a tie between Miriam and Donatello closer than the "marriage-bond" – the result of this criminal transgression – and a sympathy that "annihilated all other ties" (4: 174). The marriage has truly been consecrated in blood.

While most critics emphasize the moral aspects of "The Faun's Transformation" (the title Hawthorne gives to the pivotal chapter 19), Hawthorne also represents a psychological and physical metamorphosis in which gender and sexuality come violently together. He does not represent a closeted homoeroticism in Donatello so much as he explores a male subjectivity not constructed in relation to any gendered object until, that is, the traumatic murder scene on the Tarpeian Rock. Donatello's youthful sexuality, which does not seem to be directed at any single love object, is heterosexualized through the murder that Miriam encourages him to commit. Donatello grows up almost spontaneously into a heterosexual male in the act of murdering another man – violently repressing the possibility of homoerotic desire and so transforming himself into a man who instantaneously enjoys a "union," born in passion, "cemented with blood," and marked by increasing "loathsomeness" (4: 175), with the woman for whom he has killed this other man.

Donatello's murder of the model and the bond he forms with Miriam over the other man's dead body put those two characters on track to end up with each other. Hawthorne continues to interest himself, however, in Kenyon's personal and artistic relationship with the Faun. The scene at Monte Beni, in which Kenyon fulfills his desire to sculpt Donatello's bust – a scene of a man sculpting a man – brings that relationship to a climax. By sculpting Donatello's head, Kenyon has created a second, decapitated Faun – that is, a Faun separated from its body. The conflict between mind and body loomed large for nineteenth-century writers, and Hawthorne explores that dualism here in an especially graphic way – with Donatello in the flesh seated beside his sculpted double. Kenyon's purpose is to make the head fit the body – to solve the sticky problem of relating the "moist, brown clay" and the "features of Donatello" (4: 271), the problem Hawthorne confronted in the shape of Hiram Powers's Washington. Kenyon struggles manfully, despite "brooding much and often upon his host's personal characteristics" (4: 270), precisely because Donatello's "inner man" (4: 271) seems so resistant to the sort of fossilizing process that sculpture represents. Not only can Kenyon not make the countenance the "index of the mind within"; he cannot even catch a glimpse of a "genuine and permanent trait" (4: 270). In desperation, Kenyon surrenders control, simply letting his hands "work, uncontrolled, with the clay," flattering himself that the "true image of his friend was about to emerge." Even this doesn't work right away; the result to Donatello's perception is "like looking a stranger in the face" (4: 271).

Only when Kenyon falls into a "passion with the stubborn image, and cared not what might happen to it," does he succeed. He "compressed, elongated, widened, and otherwise altered the features of the bust, in mere recklessness," until Donatello, catching his hand, cries out, "Stop!" "Let it remain so!" (4: 272). Hawthorne included many passages illustrating the creative process in his works, but this one is surely one of the most provocative. It reminds us of the "Squeeze of the Hand" chapter in Melville's *Moby-Dick*, in which Ishmael describes squeezing spermaceti with the other members of the crew. That scene, too, ends in a kind of ecstasy in which the men end up squeezing each other's hands. Here, Kenyon is working with clay, only a replica of Donatello, but the homosocial and homoerotic feelings seem very similar. Kenyon's ecstasy seems to be self-policed, because in his "accidental handling of the clay, entirely independent of his own will," he has given the face a "distorted and violent look, combining animal fierceness with intelligent hatred" (4: 272). He has recreated the expression that Miriam and Hilda "beheld at that terrible moment" when Donatello held the model over the verge of the Tarpeian Rock. What Kenyon brings forth, in other words, is an erotically charged Donatello, but constructed heterosexually through Miriam's desiring look not into a male friend but into a jealous lover.

Not surprisingly, when Kenyon recovers his consciousness and recognizes what he has done, he quickly applies his "artful fingers to the clay, and compelled the bust to dismiss the expression that had so startled them both." "It were a sin," he exclaims, "shocked at his own casual production," to "let the clay, which bears your features, harden into a look like that" (4: 272). Having enjoyed the tactile pleasure of playing with another man's sculpted body, Kenyon atones for the "sin" he feels he has committed with his "loving hands" (4: 273).

Kenyon does not feel conflicted as an artist only when he sculpts such a male figure, of course. His most successful sculpture, created when he achieved a similar state of "passive sensibility," is a clay model of Cleopatra that Hawthorne based on a sculpture by William Wetmore Story. A near perfect embodiment of the sculptor's ambivalence toward women, the statue is also an interesting composite of values that are often mutually exclusive. Both "implacable as a stone, and cruel as fire" (4: 127), Cleopatra stands in "marvellous repose," yet reveals a "great, smouldering furnace, deep down in the woman's heart." Something like Miriam's vengeful portraits of women, moreover, the Cleopatra possesses such "latent energy and fierceness" that it appears "she might spring upon you like a tigress, and stop the very breath that you were now drawing, midway in your throat" (4: 126).

Just as Donatello's bust mediates Kenyon's relationship to Donatello himself, the Cleopatra offers a sounding board by which Hawthorne tests the relationship between Kenyon and Miriam. When Miriam questions the sculptor about the process through which the Cleopatra came into being, she recognizes a process akin to her own, and she concludes – mistakenly, it turns out – that Kenyon may be a good candidate for a confidence. "Were you not afraid to touch her, as she grew more and more towards hot life, beneath your hand?" she wonders. Kenyon does not answer that provocative question, but he does acknowledge that he doesn't quite know how he came to form such "hot life" with his hands. "I kindled a great fire within my mind," he tells her, "and threw in the material – as Aaron threw the gold of the Israelites into the furnace – and, in the midmost heat, uprose Cleopatra, as you see her" (4: 127). Identifying with him through the medium of a woman that must remind both of them of her, Miriam asks Kenyon to be her friend and to hear a secret from her heart that "burns" and "tortures" her. Kenyon struggles with his answer, and even though he invites her to consider him a brother, he recognizes but does not say that he fears the prospect of offering her so much sympathy. Miriam reads his reluctance, which angers her. "You are as cold and pitiless as your own marble," she bristles, and she tells him to keep his sympathy. "You can do nothing for me, unless you petrify me into a marble companion for your Cleopatra there; and I am not of her sisterhood, I do assure you!" (4: 129).

If Hawthorne seems to flirt with the idea that Kenyon finds himself, as a sculptor at least, in a triangular relationship with Donatello and Miriam, he eliminates the male leg of the triangle toward the end of the novel – pairing off his four characters into conventional couples. He had solved a similar problem posed by multiple relationships in *The Blithedale Romance*, of course, as Hollingsworth and Priscilla marry, while Coverdale implausibly claims that he, too, was in love with Priscilla. He had killed off the fourth member of his character quartet (Zenobia) in the earlier novel, using old material from his notebook.

Variations on this pattern characterize each of his novels. Hawthorne begins with characters with radical potential in one form or other – Hester's sexual radicalism, Holgrave's reformist zeal, Zenobia's feminism and Hollingsworth's philanthropy, Miriam's feminist painting. To some degree, each character's radicalism threatens – or promises – to move the narrative into a radical path. Hester promotes a utopian ideal to Dimmesdale that involves throwing off their names and identities and taking new ones somewhere in the wilderness. Holgrave might put his reformist ideas into practice, subverting the established order of society in the process, and certainly overturning the laws of owner-ship that have enabled the Pyncheons to cheat his family (the Maules) out of their property. Zenobia might fulfill Hester's forecast of a new relationship between men and women in the nineteenth-century society that was already rife with feminist agitation. Hollingsworth might pair up with Coverdale in a homosocial camaraderie of democratic philanthropy. Miriam might go on to fulfill her promise as feminist painter, encouraging Kenyon to develop his own potential for depicting alternative sexualities in his sculpture. Instead, of course, Hawthorne forecloses upon these possibilities by directing each narrative into a conventional track – the *liebestod* ending of *The Scarlet Letter* (Hester and Dimmesdale buried side by side), the conventional marriages between Holgrave and Phoebe, Hollingsworth and Priscilla, Kenyon and Hilda.

Ironically in *The Marble Faun*, Miriam, arguably the most successful artist in the work of art, supervises the conclusion of the novel. At the end of *The Scarlet Letter* Hester seemed wholly dependent upon Dimmesdale for vitality. When he failed her, she assumed the form of cold marble (1: 240, 244). Similarly, despite her much greater freedom of expression, Zenobia also was objectified into a frozen posture of hostility at the end of *The Blithedale Romance*. But Miriam operates very actively in the final scenes of *The Marble Faun*. She arranges for the temporary separation of Hilda and Kenyon, as if she would make one last effort to educate them in the "foreign" values associated with Rome. Hilda enters the Cenci castle, where she comes face to face with the world of violent legend that lurks in Miriam's background. (Hawthorne identifies Miriam with Beatrice Cenci, executed for the murder of her father, who had abused and even committed incest with her, according to tradition.) Through her seclusion in the Cenci castle, Hilda has a chance to develop more sympathy for Miriam. This she does not do, of course. Kenyon has two important experiences – first on the Campagna and then at the Roman carnival.

As he searches for Hilda in the Roman countryside, Kenyon discovers instead a statue of the *Venus de' Medici*. Although Hawthorne encountered the statue in the Uffizi Museum in Florence, in the novel he describes it as being still in the ground. Miriam and Donatello have discovered and unearthed it, and it becomes a tangible reminder of the passionate, sensual art that Kenyon has only rarely created. In its dismantled state, it is a three-dimensional puzzle that tests Kenyon's ability to imagine a fully embodied woman. As Nina Baym points out, the "order in which Kenyon puts together the pieces of this shattered work – torso, arms, head – represents the progressive embodiment of the fundamental erotic force, an epitome of the artistic process of creation" (*Shape*, 245). As he reassembles the fractured *Venus*, he creates a "magical" effect, a perfect, holistic image of "Womanhood," another work of art informed by a kind of sacred fire (4: 423–24). Resembling his Cleopatra much more than Hilda's diminutive hand, the *Venus* that Miriam and Donatello place in Kenyon's way tests his ability to unite the objectified and fragmented parts of a woman into a unified whole. The scene offers another example of Hawthorne's interest in the way that looking at and touching sculpture reveals and challenges the desire that the viewer brings to the process.

In the end, however, Kenyon cannot assimilate the *Venus's* energy because he does not wish to include the statue's sensuality in his image of woman. He resembles Theodore in Zenobia's legend in this respect. He allows the *Venus* to create her creator only momentarily before, like Hawthorne in the Custom House with the scarlet letter, he drops an object too "hot" to handle. He cannot follow Miriam's advice that he respond to the statue's "frightening" aspect, he says, because "imagination and the love of art have both died" out of him (4: 427).

Having failed to heed the lesson of the Campagna, Kenyon finds himself in an even more dynamic world of art when he goes to the Roman carnival. Recalling the revelry in *The Blithedale Romance*, the carnival represents a dynamic, alternative form of performance art whose "material" is human character. Hawthorne loved to write such crowd scenes in which individual identities and social order destabilize, if only briefly, before order is restored. In *The Marble Faun*, which has already explored the possibility of human transformation in the form of cross-species identification (in the case of Donatello and the Faun), Hawthorne emphasizes the interracial and inter-species forms that human identity can assume: "Clowns and parti-colored harlequins; orang-outangs; bear-headed, bull-headed, and dog-headed individuals; faces that would have been human, but for their enormous noses; one terrific creature, with a visage right in the centre of his breast; and all other imaginable kinds of monstrosity and exaggeration" (4: 446). Like Coverdale or Goodman Brown, Kenyon feels threatened by these examples of the wild forms that human character can assume. Much as Coverdale is threatened with an arrow through the heart by Zenobia, Kenyon's experience is climaxed when he is "killed" by a "gigantic female figure" who sprays him with lime dust and thus transforms him into one of his own dusty white statues (4: 445, 446). Symbolically, he represents living proof that, as Miriam had asserted, he is as "cold and pitiless" as his own marble.

In most of Hawthorne's narratives, a woman is "captured" in the form of a statue, so that her dangerous features may be rendered harmless while more benign qualities are idealized. In *The Marble Faun* that process certainly occurs in the case of Hilda's marble hand, but Miriam seems to escape such a fate. The art objects with which she is associated all burn with some inner fire. By the same token, the novel itself originated from the idea of a statue, the *Faun* of Praxiteles, coming to life, and Hawthorne works an interesting variation on the Pygmalion myth in the experiences of his two male characters, Donatello and Kenyon. Under Miriam's influence, for better or worse, according to one's judgment of his "fall," the Faun comes to have a fully human life, while Kenyon, like Hilda, undergoes the process in reverse. Both characters resist implication in Miriam's experience. Kenyon refuses to be another Donatello and so hardens from within. As an artist he prefers Hilda's marble hand to the sculpted Donatello's or the Venus's "frightening" vitality. As a man he is himself gradually transformed into a cold and pitiless statue.

Hawthorne had already developed this idea in his early story "The Man of Adamant" (1837), whose protagonist, Richard Digby, so hardens his heart against other men and women, that he goes off to live in a cave, where the metaphor of "hardening" comes true and he becomes petrified (a man of adamant) as a gigantic statue. Hawthorne developed the idea further in his last major tale, "Ethan Brand" (1850), which features a character who spends his life searching for the Unpardonable Sin, only to discover it in his own hard heart. Ethan Brand throws himself into a lime kiln at the end of the story, reducing himself to "fragments" (11: 102). In a moment of recognition before his suicide, Brand acknowledges that he has sacrificed the heart for the intellect. His heart "had withered – had contracted – had hardened – had perished! It had ceased to partake of the universal throb." In language that anticipates Walt Whitman's apostrophe to the love of comrades only five years later in "Song of Myself," Brand recognizes that he "was no longer a brother-man, opening the chambers or the dungeons of our common nature by the key of holy sympathy, which gave him a right to share in all its secrets; he was now a cold observer, looking on mankind as the subject of his experiment, and, at length, converting man and woman to be his puppets, and pulling the wires that moved them to such degrees of crime as were demanded for his study" (11: 99). "Ethan Brand" takes place in the Berkshires, and it was once considered a reference to Herman Melville and the image of literary camaraderie he suggested to Hawthorne. "Your heart beat in my ribs and mine in yours," Melville had written upon receiving Hawthorne's letter about reading *Moby-Dick* (*Correspondence*, 212). Hawthorne composed the tale, however, before he moved to Lenox.

Hawthorne has Hollingsworth offer Miles Coverdale a similarly intimate friendship in *The Blithedale Romance*. "Strike hands with me," Hollingsworth urges; "and, from this moment, you shall never again feel the languor and vague wretchedness of an indolent or half-occupied man" (3: 124). But Coverdale perceives Hollingsworth's offer as a "great, black ugliness of sin," and he convinces himself that, if he had touched Hollingsworth's "extended hand," his "magnetism would have penetrated me with his own conception of all those matters" (3: 124). Earlier, in response to Coverdale's attempt to introduce the ideas of Charles Fourier into a discussion with Hollingsworth, the latter had exploded, "I never will forgive this fellow! He has committed the Unpardonable Sin! For what more monstrous iniquity could the Devil himself contrive, than to choose the selfish principle – the principle of all human wrong, the very blackness of man's heart" (3: 50).

The association of Unpardonable Sin with male friendship has a place in "Ethan Brand," when Ethan finds himself alone with the lime-kiln operator, Bartram. When Bartram's son Joe leaves for the village to inform everyone of Brand's return, Brand feels "that the little fellow's presence had been a barrier between his guest and himself, and that he must now deal, heart to heart, with a man who, on his own confession, had committed the only crime for which Heaven could afford no mercy. That crime, in its indistinct blackness, seemed to overshadow him. The lime-burner's own sins rose up within him, and made his memory riotous with a throng of evil shapes that asserted their kindred with the Master Sin, whatever it might be, which it was within the scope of man's corrupted nature to conceive and cherish. They were all of one family; they went to and fro between his breast and Ethan Brand's, and carried dark greetings from one to the other" (11: 88). The language and imagery in these three texts (Melville's letters, *The Blithedale Romance*, and "Ethan Brand") all reflect an effort on Hawthorne's part to come to terms with the sort of friendship Melville offered him.

Kenyon, of course, is nowhere near as "adamant" as Ethan Brand, although being "killed" into a statue by a gigantic female figure does place him in a similar situation. More important, Kenyon judges Miriam and Donatello harshly and prefers to know as little as possible about their experience. He is unruffled by the "feverish dream" of the carnival (4: 44–46), and as soon as the masqueraders leave his haunted mind, "as dreams and spectres do," he doggedly pursues his "quest" for Hilda (4: 447). In declaring their separation from Europe and from art, they dissociate themselves from Miriam and her experience. When they see her for the final time, it is as if she "stood on the other side of a fathomless abyss, and warned them from its verge" (4: 461).

In contrast to Hilda, Kenyon remains at least potentially sympathetic to Miriam and Donatello and their transgressive relationship. In a scene at the end of the novel, in fact, he broaches the idea of moral relativism and the concept of the Fortunate Fall (the idea that Donatello's "fall" from innocence, like Adam's, was fortunate because, paradoxically, a prerequisite for his redemption). He admits being perplexed that Donatello appears "elevated" by sin, and wonders if sin is "merely an element of human education, through which we struggle to a higher and purer state than we could otherwise have attained" (4: 460). Hilda expresses shock "beyond words" at the idea, and Kenyon begs her forgiveness for letting his mind wander so "wild and wide" (4: 460). He implores her to guide and protect him from his own wayward thoughts with the "white wisdom" that "clothes" her "as with a celestial garment" (4: 460–61). Whatever his earlier sympathy for Miriam, the open-mindedness that produced the Cleopatra and earned her confidence, Kenyon has lost it as surely as "imagination and a love of art" have died out of him.

The novel draws rapidly to a close. Whereas Coverdale loves Priscilla from a distance at the end of *The Blithedale Romance* – presumably, without her knowing anything of the feelings he claims to have – Kenyon wins "gentle Hilda's shy affection." We suspect, in view of her imminent canonization "as a household Saint, in the light of her husband's fireside" (4: 461), that the former sculptor will see little more of her than the dainty hand whose impression he stole in a weak moment. The purifying role that Hilda played as a copyist of the Old Masters will be transferred to the home. In this role, as I noted, Hilda is a reincarnation of Phoebe in *The House of the Seven Gables*. Earlier, during a tour of St. Peter's, Kenyon had imagined an ideal "nuptial home" for the two of them in the sanctity of the church. What a "delicious life it would be," he said, "if a colony of people with delicate lungs (or merely with delicate fancies) could take up their abode in this ever-mild and tranquil air! These architectural tombs of the Popes might serve for dwellings, and each brazen sepulchral door-way would become a domestic threshold" (4: 369). In an extraordinary fantasy, Kenyon imagines a lover asking his mistress to share his tomb. Perhaps indicating the atmosphere of his own nuptial home, he says fondly, "What a life would be theirs, Hilda, in their marble Eden!" (4: 369). Kenyon's vision of wedded bliss seems entirely appropriate to his character and his penchant for turning "feverish men into cool, quiet marble."

Hawthorne published *The Marble Faun* in 1860, four years before his death. It would prove to be the last work of fiction he completed. He had begun an English novel entitled "The Ancestral Footstep" during the years he spent in England, putting that work aside when he became so captivated by the *Faun* of Praxiteles he discovered in Rome that he felt compelled to begin a new novel on the spot. He made various efforts to complete the English narrative. The so-called *American Claimant Manuscripts* collected in the Centenary Edition of his works include three different versions, "The Ancestral Footstep," "Etherege," and "Grimshawe." Some time after returning to America, Hawthorne decided to abandon the effort. Instead, he tried to write a novel set in Concord at the time of the Revolutionary War, but in this case, too, he left behind three sets of manuscript fragments ("Septimius Felton," Septimius Norton," and "The Dolliver Romance"), now collected as the *Elixir of Life Manuscripts*. If Hawthorne flirted with the idea of immortality, he did so under the prospect, which he may or may have realized, of approaching death.

Chapter 5

Hawthorne's critics

Hawthorne has been a subject of serious study ever since Henry James's 1879 book (*Hawthorne*) in the American Men of Letters series, and critics have approached his writing from many angles. Most recent studies have used historical approaches, emphasizing either his use of older historical settings, particularly seventeenth-century Puritan New England, or his connections to the nineteenth-century world in which he wrote. Hawthorne knew his history, but the trend in Hawthorne scholarship, as it is generally in American literary studies, is toward stressing the cultural context offered by the politically volatile world in which he lived. The decade of the 1990s was dominated by New Historicist analyses of Hawthorne and his writing that place him within that culture, often unflatteringly, because of his relatively conservative views toward questions of gender, class, and race. More recent criticism seems to be taking a more balanced view.

Biography

The most thorough modern biography is James R. Mellow's *Nathaniel Hawthorne in His Times* (1980). As his title suggests, Mellow pays attention to the historical and social context of Hawthorne's experience, and he provides detailed accounts of events in Hawthorne's life. Mellow's biography overshadowed Arlin Turner's *Nathaniel Hawthorne*, published in the same year, but Turner also emphasizes the connections between Hawthorne's writing and his culture. Since Mellow's and Turner's, most biographical treatments of Hawthorne have become more pointedly focused. Edwin Haviland Miller's *Salem Is My Dwelling Place* (1991) focuses on Hawthorne's personality, emotions, and family relationships. Hawthorne's early tale, "The Gentle Boy," offers Miller a paradigm for a Freudian analysis of Hawthorne's anxiety about his sexuality, his poverty, attractive young women and men. Miller's biography is best known for his account of Hawthorne's relationship with Herman Melville, which he casts in homoerotic terms. Most famously, Miller argued that Melville made an "advance" to Hawthorne that caused the two writers to become estranged in 1851.

T. Walter Herbert's *Dearest Beloved* (1993) is a psycho-cultural family biography and New Historicist exposé of the "torments intrinsic to the domestic ideal" that dominated nineteenth-century life. Herbert creates a family portrait "teeming with covert sexual politics," in which the Hawthornes' unresolved childhood traumas visit themselves upon their three children. Herbert keys each of four sections to one of the major romances and ingeniously interprets the conversation between life and art that such juxtaposition establishes. His best section involves *The Marble Faun*, the climactic family romance because of the psychic forces and characters that surfaced during the Hawthornes' Roman visit.

"We are always finding new Hawthornes," William Dean Howells wrote, in a passage Brenda Wineapple quotes near the end of her recent biography, *Hawthorne: A Life*, "but the illusion soon wears away, and then we perceive that they were not Hawthornes at all" (380). Wineapple's "new Hawthorne" does not reduce easily to a single role or identity – in contrast to the "new Hawthornes" discovered by Miller and Herbert. Wineapple might be considered the biographical realist, writing between the two poles of biographical naturalism – the psychological determinist (Miller) on the one hand, the environmental or social determinist (Herbert) on the other. As I noted in chapter 2, Wineapple's biography is especially valuable for its treatment of Hawthorne's politics and his conflicted but not unusual attitudes toward race, slavery, and abolition.

Other important biographical treatments of Hawthorne include Gloria C. Erlich's *Family Themes and Hawthorne's Fiction* (1984). Erlich emphasizes Hawthorne's early childhood experiences after his father's death, when his mother (Elizabeth Hathorne) moved him and his two sisters into the Manning family home and he came under the influence of his maternal uncle, Robert Manning. She stresses three major themes: "maternal deprivation, paternal loss, and avuncular domination" (xvii). In *The Salem World of Nathaniel Hawthorne* (1998), Margaret B. Moore focuses on Hawthorne's Salem environment, his early education and religious background. Particularly useful are her description of Salem's black population and her assessment of Hawthorne's Democratic politics. Philip McFarland, *Hawthorne in Concord* (2004), describes Hawthorne's three residencies in Concord – the honeymoon period of 1842–45, the brief period after he bought the Wayside from Bronson Alcott (1852–53), and then the last years of his life, after his return from seven years in Europe (1860–64). For biographical accounts of Hawthorne's time in Europe, Raymona E. Hull's *Nathaniel Hawthorne: The English Experience* (1980) provides expanded coverage of Hawthorne's English years and can be supplemented by Bryan Homer's *An American Liaison: Leamington Spa and the Hawthornes* (1998).

Criticism

In the years after World War II American literature scholars struggled to declare the independence of American literature from an English literary tradition. Hawthorne, whose writing had never been out of favor, helped the cause. Echoing Melville's seminal essay, "Hawthorne and His Mosses" (1850), D. H. Lawrence, in *Studies in Classic American Literature* (1923), claimed that the "blue-eyed darling Nathaniel knew disagreeable things in his inner soul" but was "careful to send them out in disguise" (83). In 1944, F. O. Matthiessen's groundbreaking *American Renaissance* established a pantheon of five male writers, Emerson, Thoreau, Hawthorne, Melville, and Whitman, and defined a remarkable moment in American literary history (1850–55), a brief period coincident with Hawthorne's most prolific publication (as *The Scarlet Letter*, *The House of the Seven Gables*, *The Blithedale Romance*, and several other works saw print during that half-decade). In *The American Adam* (1955) R. W. B. Lewis declared the opening scene of *The Scarlet Letter* to be the paradigmatic "dramatic image" in American literature, because "all that was dark and treacherous in the American situation became exposed" (111). Early scholars looked for something distinctively American about American writing, including Hawthorne's. For Richard Chase in *The American Novel and Its Tradition* (1957), Hawthorne figured as one of several nineteenth-century American writers (Cooper, Poe, and Melville being others) who wrote "romances" rather than novels. In contrast to the English novel of manners, the American romance, in Chase's view, could be characterized by its "freedom from the requirements of verisimilitude, development, and continuity; a tendency towards melodrama and idyl; a more or less formal abstractness and, on the other hand, a tendency to plunge into the underside of consciousness; a willingness to abandon moral questions or to ignore the spectacle of man in society, or to consider these things only indirectly or abstractly" (ix). Hawthorne's famous description in "The Custom-House" preface to *The Scarlet Letter* of a "neutral territory, somewhere between the real world and fairy-land, where the Actual and the Imaginary may meet, and each imbue itself with the nature of the other" (1: 36), seemed to declare independence from the commonplace in the terms that Chase described – partly because Hawthorne set the novel so far in the past, partly because he embellished the action with supernatural elements (the meteoric scarlet A, the ambiguous mark on Dimmesdale's chest). Terence Martin, *Nathaniel Hawthorne* (1983), also emphasized what he called the "neutral ground" of Hawthorne's fiction: "The difficulty of creating fiction in the 'broad and simple daylight' of his native land (where experience, no matter how limited, would be engaged and encumbered) encouraged Hawthorne to cultivate the resources of the haunted mind which gave him access to a frightening world of disengaged experience" (47). And in *The Romance in America* (1969), Joel Porte opened his chapter on Hawthorne by declaring, "It is no exaggeration to say that without Hawthorne there could be no firm theory of American romance" (95), and he went on to cite Hawthorne's "consistently expressed concern with that neutral territory" as the foundation of the theory.

Frederick Crews's *The Sins of the Fathers: Hawthorne's Psychological Themes* (1966), a paradigm-shifting book on Hawthorne in the 1960s, has influenced many Hawthorne studies over the past forty years. Crews's Freudian approach to Hawthorne grew logically out of the emphasis on Hawthorne as a romancer and a writer, as Lawrence had said, who "knew disagreeable things in his inner soul" that he sent out "in disguise." Crews wrote against earlier views of Hawthorne as a "dogmatic moralist," arguing instead that Hawthorne was a "self-divided, self-tormented man" (7) whose fiction is marked by psychological and moral ambiguity and whose plots feature a "return of the repressed" (17). He emphasized Hawthorne's secret attraction to powerful forces of rebellion against repressive paternal authority. Even though Crews later questioned the reductionist tendency of the Freudian paradigm with which he worked, his psychological study of Hawthorne's fiction has had enormous influence on critics and biographers alike. In *Using Lacan, Reading Fiction* (1991), James Mellard updated psychoanalytic approaches to Hawthorne, especially to *The Scarlet Letter*, which he considers "an almost uniquely Lacanian work of fiction" because of the connection between the letter and identity (70). Hawthorne's four major characters (Pearl, Hester, Chillingworth, Dimmesdale) represent "versions" of Lacanian subjectivity (70).

Not every critic has agreed with the romance/psychoanalytic approach to Hawthorne's writing. In *Hawthorne's View of the Artist* (1962), Millicent Bell described a counter-Romantic Hawthorne who looked with "suspicion upon the queen of Romantic faculties, that occult perspicacity which enables the artist to pierce the externals of his fellow creature, laying bare the heart's most intimate fears and desires" (7). Without employing a Freudian or psychoanalytic paradigm, in *Nathaniel Hawthorne and the Truth of Dreams* (1979) Rita Gollin examined Hawthorne from a psychological standpoint, but she asserted that Hawthorne "understood daydreaming as the Scottish Common Sense philosophers did: the mind is simultaneously aware of its own operations and its experience of the outer world; the imagination can operate freely; but since the will retains control, unpleasant thoughts cannot gain dominion" (74). Kenneth Dauber, *Rediscovering Hawthorne* (1977), also disagreed with the romantic tradition of Hawthorne criticism. He discounts Hawthorne's "visionary" aspects, whose emphasis makes him a "minor Melville" (19), in favor of a structuralist approach that discovers often contradictory stories layered one upon the other. "Rappaccini's Daughter," for example, includes an innocent-girl-victimized story and an innocent-boy-seduced story; the "tales reside on the same printed spot, as it were, but follow independent logics" (31).

Hawthorne is a notoriously ambiguous writer, and his skepticism about our ability to obtain absolute knowledge is reflected in many of his works. The Puritans' effort to assign a single meaning to the scarlet letter and to stabilize that meaning for all time offers a good example. Hawthorne's ambiguity has made him a good candidate for deconstructive approaches to his writing. In *Hawthorne and History* (1991), for example, J. Hillis Miller examines a single text, "The Minister's Black Veil," and the theory of history and historical knowledge that may be inferred from it. "The veil is the type and symbol of the fact that all signs are potentially unreadable, or that the reading of them is potentially unverifiable" (97). In other words, there is no way to "get behind the veil" or any other historical object of investigation to "find out what is really going on back there" (99). As Hawthorne represents it, history does not remain "safely stored up in traces, texts, memorials, records, vestiges, or material artifacts that can then later on be deciphered by future generations as the means of access to the original happening as it really happened" (113). As historian, Miller's Hawthorne appears almost post-modern in his skeptical view of knowledge. John T. Irwin included Hawthorne in *American Hieroglyphics* (1980), which takes its cue from the nineteenth-century fascination with the Egyptian hieroglyphics but then expands to include many hieroglyphical objects. Focusing on the scarlet letter, Irwin concludes: "The post-Kantian awareness that what a man knows is not an objective external world but simply the internal structure of his own mind projected upon an essentially indeterminate ground, the feeling of being trapped in the self, the sense of the shattering of all absolutes because of the loss of objective knowledge – these are what the concept of the hieroglyphic emblem evokes for Hawthorne" (241).

In *Secrets and Sympathy* (1988), Gordon Hutner also focuses on what is not said and not known in Hawthorne's novels, but he does not emphasize unknowability. In fact, he finds Hawthorne's interest in sympathy – as in his famous longing in "The Custom-House" for the "one heart and mind of perfect sympathy" (1: 3) – to offer a solution to the skepticism about knowledge that Irwin and other deconstructionist critics discover in Hawthorne's writing.

Hutner notes that each of the four major novels includes many secrets, including foundational secrets without which each narrative would be virtually impossible to conceive (Dimmesdale's identity as Pearl's father, Holgrave's identity as a Maule, Coverdale's love for Priscilla, the identity of Miriam's model). Whereas Hutner finds sympathy offering a kind of deep structure through which characters can communicate honestly with one another, Kenneth Marc Harris, *Hypocrisy and Self-Deception in Hawthorne's Fiction* (1988), takes a different view. "A census of all the inhabitants of Hawthorne's imagined world," he asserts, "would certainly result in the finding that the overwhelming majority are hypocrites, self-deceivers, or both" (ix).

Generic (romance) and psychoanalytic approaches are ahistorical, at least in the broadest sense, and critical approaches to Hawthorne have certainly swerved back into historical tracks during the past twenty years. Approaching Hawthorne historically can mean several different things, of course. The traditional way of thinking of Hawthorne as a historical writer involves examining his knowledge of history and American culture, but most recent historicists take a different approach. Hawthorne set many of his tales, as well as *The Scarlet Letter*, in seventeenth-century Massachusetts – usually in Salem or Boston – but recent scholars suggest that even these fictional works have been inscribed with their nineteenth-century cultural context.

Most of the recent historical studies of Hawthorne emphasize his political and social attitudes, and for the most part they express little sympathy for Hawthorne's views. The most influential, Sacvan Bercovitch's *The Office of "The Scarlet Letter"* (1991), exemplifies New Historicist cultural studies. Bercovitch seeks to "repoliticize" *The Scarlet Letter* (xvii) by examining its "profound ideological engagement" (xviii), and he focuses on Hester's return to Boston in the novel's epilogue. He explains that return and its political implications, particularly Hester's "conversion to the letter," by reading *The Scarlet Letter* as a "subtle and devastating critique of radicalism" (6) that teaches us finally to "embrace gradualism and consensus" (17). Particularly influential has been Bercovitch's application of these ideas to the issue of nineteenth-century abolitionism, for he finds Hawthorne to be a purveyor of "thick propaganda" (89) in which the existence of slavery figures as a necessary evil, or stage, in America's progressive evolution (87).

Both Jean Fagan Yellin and Nancy Bentley explore Hawthorne's relationship to slavery and abolitionism by decoding subtexts in novels that keep such connections hidden. In *Women and Sisters* (1989) and in several related essays, Yellin demonstrates Hawthorne's knowledge of the slave trade and illustrates links between *The Scarlet Letter* and the abolitionist movement. She concludes, however, that Hawthorne rejects the liberationist discourse of anti-slavery women and "endorses patriarchal notions" (126). In *The Ethnography of Manners* (1995) Bentley explores connections between fauns and slaves in *The Marble Faun*, and through the mediating concept of primitivism, she shows how contemporaneous issues of race and race classification, which are prominent in Hawthorne's Italian novel, would have resonated with significance for American readers on the eve of the Civil War.

Most studies of Hawthorne and history consider American connections, but a few scholars have explored Hawthorne's interest in foreign affairs. Frederick Newberry, *Hawthorne's Divided Loyalties* (1987), analyzes Hawthorne's career-long interest in England, concluding that Hawthorne tried to recover an aesthetic inheritance that Americans lost when they achieved political independence from England. In *European Revolutions and the American Literary Renaissance* (1988) Larry Reynolds discusses the effect (a reactionary one) that the Italian Revolution of 1849, as well as the English Civil War of 1642–49 and the first French Revolution of 1789, had on *The Scarlet Letter*. Luther Luedtke, *Nathaniel Hawthorne and the Romance of the Orient* (1989), also focuses on Hawthorne's knowledge of foreign culture and history – in this case, a fascination with the Orient that developed from his extensive reading (especially in Eastern travel literature and *The Arabian Nights*). Like Reynolds, he presents a Hawthorne much more aware of world history and culture than most scholars have appreciated. Evan Carton, *"The Marble Faun": Hawthorne's Transformations* (1992), takes a different tack and one more common among New Historicist scholars – emphasizing how even a "foreign" setting can be inscribed with American political and cultural issues, such as "separate spheres" ideology and the racial tensions (inscribed in the ambiguous racial identities of Miriam and Donatello) of pre-Civil War America. And in *Practicing Romance: Narrative Form and Cultural Engagement in Hawthorne's Fiction* (1992) Richard Millington synthesizes Freudian psychoanalysis, New Historicism, reader-response theory, and other critical methodologies to deliver fresh insights into the interplay of individual and society in Hawthorne's fiction. Millington argues that the "neutral territory" which Hawthorne defines in "The Custom-House" represents a contested space in which he can perform revisionary cultural work.

Other critics explore Hawthorne's relation to particular nineteenth-century social movements. Taylor Stoehr, *Hawthorne's Mad Scientists* (1978), analyzes Hawthorne's interest in nineteenth-century "pseudosciences," mesmerism, physiognomy and phrenology, homeopathy, associationism, spiritualism, feminism, and even prison reform, and he examines the influence of such "isms" on *The House of the Seven Gables* and *The Blithedale Romance* in particular. Samuel Chase Coale, *Mesmerism and Hawthorne* (1998), examines the mesmerist–spiritualist "craze" in mid-nineteenth-century American culture and then relates it to Hawthorne's four major novels and selected tales.

While the trend in Hawthorne scholarship is a focus on how nineteenth-century political and social issues inscribe themselves on texts, there are many examples of an older historical approach to the question of Hawthorne's historical knowledge. Michael Colacurcio, *The Province of Piety: Moral History in Hawthorne's Early Tales* (1984), provides exhaustive, erudite analyses of selected tales (most notably, "The Gentle Boy," "The Minister's Black Veil," "Young Goodman Brown," and the four "Legends of the Province House") in the context of their seventeenth-century and eighteenth-century settings. Colacurcio's Hawthorne is "our first significant intellectual historian" (3), who "carried on a life-long dialectic with the historical 'thesis' of American Puritanism" (1).

Other valuable studies of Hawthorne's use of historical background materials include Michael Davitt Bell's *Hawthorne and the Historical Romance of New England* (1971), John P. McWilliams, Jr.'s *Hawthorne, Melville, and the American Character* (1984), and George Dekker's *The American Historical Romance* (1987). Situating Hawthorne within a context of more than two dozen nineteenth-century romances about Puritan New England, Bell interests himself particularly in the way these historical romances represent a "battle between embryonic democracy and decadent authoritarianism" (8). Both McWilliams and Dekker examine linear connections among seventeenth-century, eighteenth-century, and nineteenth-century moments in American history, especially the relationship of the Puritan experiment to the American Revolution and then to the progressive movements associated with Jacksonian America. Hawthorne's tales, McWilliams believes, "constitute a thorough study of New England's development" between the time of the first settlement and the aftermath of the Revolution (25), and he traces a line from "the Puritan character" (exemplified by John Winthrop) through Revolutionary War filiopietism (associated with George Washington) to nineteenth-century American character. In his survey of historical fiction in the "Waverley" tradition established by Sir Walter Scott, Dekker also examines Hawthorne's "filiopietistic reading of history," his efforts to reconcile "regional and national loyalties by highlighting those aspects of the New England past (e.g. Puritan love of 'liberty') which could be construed to foreshadow or, like seeds, contain the future nation" (129).

In *Hawthorne's Shyness: Ethics, Politics, and the Question of Engagement* (2005), Clark Davis writes from a phenomenological viewpoint against ideologically based studies of Hawthorne, particularly those that consider him deterministically inscribed by his conservative culture. Davis wishes to refocus attention on ethical human subjects and thus on Hawthorne's engagement – and complex depiction of engagement – with ethical questions. Ideologically based critics, he says, "make little room for individual human choice" (18), much less for the notion of authorial "intention" (19). Davis does not shy away from Hawthorne's politics, but he certainly disagrees with Bercovitch and others, who find Hawthorne espousing conformity or consent. Davis's Hawthorne is a political realist: "For Hawthorne there is no easy choice between conformity and rebellion; there is instead a set of choices with political effects that are limited by ethical concerns" (81).

What Frederick Crews did for those interested in Hawthorne's psychology, Nina Baym has done for those interested in Hawthorne's relation to issues of gender and sexuality. In a remarkable series of insightful essays in the early 1970s, culminating in *The Shape of Hawthorne's Career* (1976), Baym posited a Romantic rather than Puritan or Christian Hawthorne, a man who secretly identifies with his powerful and passionate female characters as they rebel against patriarchal authority. In contrast, in her feminist study, *Nathaniel Hawthorne* (1987), Louise DeSalvo considers Hawthorne complicit with those who victimize women – e.g., Miles Coverdale in *The Blithedale Romance* and the Puritan patriarchs in *The Scarlet Letter*. DeSalvo terms the latter work a "revisionist history" (64) that "deflects attention away from the reality of Hester's utter powerlessness in the Puritan scheme" (65), and she concludes that the "universe of Hawthorne's fiction is an accurate representation of a patriarchy gone mad with misogyny" (122). I come to a conclusion closer to Baym's in three chapters of *Aesthetic Headaches* (1988), as I focus on female characters (including Hester) who refuse to be controlled by men – creating a paradigm of female empowerment and influence that can be observed in tales such as "Rappaccini's Daughter" and in each of the four major romances. Joel Pfister, in *The Production of Personal Life* (1991), historicizes Hawthornian psychology by focusing on the intersection of gender and class (especially new middle-class domestic values) in Hawthorne's fiction. He concludes that Hawthorne critiqued the "sentimental construction of 'masculine' and 'feminine' roles upon which the economic and cultural ascendancy of his class relied" (8).

Emily Miller Budick, *Engendering Romance: Women Writers and the Hawthorne Tradition* (1994), places Hawthorne at the head of a female tradition of romance writing that includes Carson McCullers, Flannery O'Connor, Toni Morrison, and Grace Paley (as well as Henry James and William Faulkner). Budick considers *The Scarlet Letter* "one of the most powerful literary critiques of the misogyny of patriarchal society" (14). Emphasizing consent rather than consensus, this tradition, as inaugurated in *The Scarlet Letter*, "has intimately to do with questions of choice and responsibility – in particular, with choosing a place within history and tradition and with assuming responsibility both for oneself and for one's progeny" (2).

In a provocative feminist study, *The Scarlet Mob of Scribblers: Rereading Hester Prynne* (2000), Jamie Barlowe criticizes Hawthorne's male critics for ignoring work by women and feminists, and she attempts to right the balance by including a "collaborative" reading of *The Scarlet Letter* that organizes much of the criticism by women that the male tradition, in her view, has excluded. One of her major contributions is an excellent chapter on the 1995 film version of *The Scarlet Letter*. Unlike many reviewers of the film, Barlowe gives director Roland Joffe considerable credit for critiquing Hawthorne's novel, especially for its marginalization of Native American Indians and African Americans.

A good example of the way scholars have moved away from examining women as symbols (of "dark" or "light" impulses) or representatives of certain ideas (e.g., feminism), the essays collected in *Hawthorne and Women: Engendering and Expanding the Hawthorne Tradition*, edited by John Idol and Melinda Ponder, focus on Hawthorne's connection with actual women. Some contributors discuss the influence of women, such as Elizabeth Peabody (John Idol), Sophia Hawthorne (Luanne Jenkins Hurst), Rose Hawthorne Lathrop (Patricia Dunlavy Valenti), Annie Fields (Rita Gollin), Mary Russell Mitford (John Idol). David Kesterson and Thomas Mitchell both examine Hawthorne's relationship with Margaret Fuller. James D. Wallace examines "Stowe and Hawthorne." Claudia Durst Johnson places Hawthorne in the context of his "literary neighbors" in Concord (especially Louisa May Alcott).

Others examine Hawthorne's influence, or at least the way his concerns find their way into later women's writing. Margaret Moore looks at Elizabeth Stoddard's *The Morgesons* for Hawthornian affinities. Patricia Marks pairs up Hilda in *The Marble Faun* and George Eliot's Dorothea Brooke in *Middlemarch*. Carol Bensick focuses on Mary (aka Mrs. Humphry) Ward's epistolary response to Hawthorne in honor of the centennial of his birth. Both Janice Milner Lasseter and Gayle Smith see Hawthorne's sketches – gloomy, realistic, detailed – as models. Lasseter explores "Hawthorne's Legacy to Rebecca Harding Davis," while Smith focuses on Sarah Orne Jewett, despite her claim that she was not a Hawthorne lover. Melissa McFarland Pennell discovers Hepzibah Pyncheon in *The House of the Seven Gables* lurking behind several of Mary Wilkins Freeman's "old maids." Melinda Ponder analyzes the role Katherine Lee Bates (author of "America the Beautiful") played in promoting Hawthorne's reputation in her 1898 anthology of American literature and several other writings. John J. Murphy analyzes Hawthorne and Willa Cather as "kindred spirits" by comparing *The Blithedale Romance* and *My Ántonia* and *The Marble Faun* and *Death Comes for the Archbishop*. Elizabeth Goodenough pairs Hawthorne and Virginia Woolf by focusing on how concepts of children inspired each writer's masterpiece (*The Scarlet Letter* and *To the Lighthouse*). Despite Emily Dickinson's few references to Hawthorne, Karen Kilcup persuasively argues that "Dickinson shares with Hawthorne a number of attitudes and images that render her familiarity with his work both likely and significant" (237). Denise Knight finds Hawthorne's influence not only in Charlotte Perkins Gilman's "Clifford's Tower," but also in the less obvious "Old Water." Monika Elbert compares *The Scarlet Letter* and Edith Wharton's *Summer* as novels of seduction that construct triangles of two men vying for one woman. John Gatta traces the influence of *The Scarlet Letter* as a "satanic pretext" for Flannery O'Connor's "Good Country People." And Franny Nudelman brings *The Scarlet Letter* and Toni Morrison's *Beloved* together for their treatment of similar family dynamics.

One of the most compelling recent books on Hawthorne is Thomas Mitchell's *Hawthorne's Fuller Mystery* (1998), which explores Hawthorne's obsession with Margaret Fuller throughout his writing career. More interested in Fuller's emotional and psychological effect on Hawthorne than in the influence of her feminist ideas, Mitchell makes a persuasive case for Fuller's inspiration of the strong, mysterious women characters in "Rappaccini's Daughter," *The Scarlet Letter*, *The Blithedale Romance*, and *The Marble Faun*. Fuller challenged Hawthorne's conception of his own gender identity, Mitchell argues, and he considers Sophia Peabody Hawthorne and Fuller the "Strophe and Antistrophe" of Hawthorne's life and art (243).

Interest in Hawthorne as a man and in his representation of male sexuality and homosexuality has become more and more common. In addition to Walter Herbert's biographical treatments of Hawthorne's manhood, David Leverenz, in *Manhood and the American Renaissance* (1989), explores Hawthorne's quarrel with nineteenth-century models of manhood, which he depicts as "aggressive, insensitive, and murderously dominant" (231). Male rivalries and a dominance–humiliation dynamic dominate Hawthorne's fiction (in "My Kinsman, Major Molineux," "Rappaccini's Daughter," and *The Scarlet Letter*, for example), culminating in the threat of homosexual rape (Coverdale by Hollingsworth) in *The Blithedale Romance*.

Questions about Hawthorne's sexual identity and especially his attitudes toward male–male relationships have most often arisen in discussion of his friendship with Herman Melville. James C. Wilson, *The Hawthorne and Melville Friendship* (1991), edited a useful collection of scholarship published before 1990 on the two writers' friendship and the ways they influenced each other's writing. Robert K. Martin and I edited a special issue of *ESQ: A Journal of the American Renaissance* (2000) devoted to the Hawthorne–Melville relationship; the issue included essays by Robert Milder ("'The Ugly Socrates': Melville,

Hawthorne, and Homoeroticism"), Thomas Mitchell ("In the Whale's Wake: Melville and *The Blithedale Romance*"), and Brenda Wineapple ("Hawthorne and Melville; or, The Ambiguities"). The most extreme view of the relationship and its effect on the subsequent fiction is Monika Mueller's *This Infinite Fraternity of Feeling: Gender, Genre, and Homoerotic Crisis in Hawthorne's "The Blithedale Romance" and Melville's "Pierre"* (1996). Hawthorne felt "dismayed and confused by Melville's sexual interest in him," Mueller argues, because it made him feel "feminized" (14), and those feelings directly influence *The Blithedale Romance*.

To Robert K. Martin's seminal 1990 article, "Hester Prynne, *C'est Moi*," we must add Scott S. Derrick's, "'A Curious Subject of Observation and Inquiry': Homoeroticism, the Body, and Authorship in Hawthorne's *The Scarlet Letter*," *Novel* 28 (1995): 308–26, and Karen L. Kilcup's "'Ourself behind Ourself, Concealed–': the Homoerotics of Reading in *The Scarlet Letter*," *ESQ* 42 (1996): 1–28. Derrick sees *The Scarlet Letter* as a complexly homophobic novel. He examines the scene in which Chillingworth accosts the sleeping Dimmesdale, using Sylvester Graham's *A Lecture to Young Men* (1834) and its various sexual phobias to interpret Dimmesdale's and Chillingworth's "symptomology" as victims of sexual disease. Kilcup not only examines same-sex relationships in the novel but also the "hide-and-seek" relationship between author and reader, which she construes as male-to-male and erotically charged.

Hawthorne has long been considered a master of the short-story form, and even though many tales consistently merit attention in books on various subjects, studies that focus exclusively on the tales and sketches continue to be published. Still valuable is Lea Bertani Vozar Newman's *A Reader's Guide to the Short Stories of Nathaniel Hawthorne* (1979), which organizes and summarizes criticism on each of Hawthorne's fifty-four short works. For a book-length study of Hawthorne's children's tales, see Laura Laffrado, *Hawthorne's Literature for Children* (1992). G. R. Thompson's *The Art of Authorial Presence: Hawthorne's Provincial Tales* (1993) represents Hawthorne as a crafty manipulator of narrative voice and "authorial presence." Central to Hawthorne's "narrative aesthetics" is the "complex nature of the foregrounded narrator as figured 'author' and his intricate relation to the structure of narrator–narratee transactions." Thompson emphasizes eight early tales, which he (re)constructs as Hawthorne's *Provincial Tales*: four "dreamvision sketches" ("The Hollow of the Three Hills," "The Wives of the Dead," "An Old Woman's Tale," "Alice Doane's Appeal") and four historical tales ("The Gray Champion," "Roger Malvin's Burial," "The Gentle Boy," "My Kinsman, Major Molineux").

Marked by ingenious wordplay and indebted theoretically to Derrida, Lacan, Heidegger, and Merleau-Ponty, John Dolis's *The Style of Hawthorne's Gaze:*

Regarding Subjectivity (1993) focuses on the visually deconstructive aspect of Hawthorne's imagination. Emphasizing almost exclusively the novels, especially *The Scarlet Letter*, Dolis offers a kaleidoscopic account of Hawthorne's "metamorphic reality" and the situational subjectivity it engenders. Hawthorne consistently honors the "reciprocity between subject and object" by destabilizing the subject–object dichotomy – a phenomenon that Dolis illustrates in a brilliant analysis of the brook-side scene in *The Scarlet Letter*. In the best attempt since Nina Baym's to demonstrate Hawthorne's thematic development, Alison Easton, in *The Making of the Hawthorne Subject* (1996), finds Hawthorne divided between two inherited theories of the human subject, Scottish Common Sense psychology and Romantic ideas of the individual. Easton traces Hawthorne's early evolution as a writer by honoring the compositional order of his works and by analyzing the "topology of self" those early works disclose, and the distinctions she makes between Hawthorne's early and late stories are especially valuable.

Increased interest in Hawthorne's embeddedness in his culture has sponsored several valuable collections that situate his writing in the context offered by various movements, as well as other contemporaneous texts. In *Understanding "The Scarlet Letter": A Student Casebook to Issues, Sources, and Historical Documents* (1995), Claudia Durst Johnson provides excerpts from seventeenth-century, nineteenth-century, and even twentieth-century documents to aid readers in developing various historical contexts for understanding the novel. Ross C. Murfin's 1991 edition of *The Scarlet Letter* provides a very useful casebook of theoretical approaches to the novel. Besides surveys of relevant criticism, the volume includes examples of psychoanalytic criticism (Joanne Feit Diehl), reader-response criticism (David Leverenz), feminist criticism (Shari Benstock), deconstruction (Michael Ragussis), and New Historicism (Sacvan Bercovitch). William E. Cain's edition (1996) of *The Blithedale Romance* includes well-chosen selections of nineteenth-century works of social philosophy (especially on utopianism and women's rights) to create a rich cultural context. Among the writers represented: Karl Marx, Friederich Engels, William Lloyd Garrison, Charles Fourier, Robert Owen, John Humphrey Noyes, Bronson and Louisa May Alcott, George Ripley, Angelina Grimké, and Margaret Fuller.

The Cambridge Companion to Nathaniel Hawthorne (2004), edited by Richard H. Millington, includes a dozen topical essays by prominent scholars, each of them coming at Hawthorne from a different cultural angle. Larry J. Reynolds examines "Hawthorne's Labors in Concord" during his first, three-year residence there. Joel Pfister analyzes "Hawthorne as Cultural Theorist." For T. Walter Herbert it is "Hawthorne and American Masculinity," while Alison

Easton surveys "Hawthorne and the Question of Women." Kristie Hamilton explores a neglected part of Hawthorne's canon in "Hawthorne, Modernity, and the Literary Sketch." Gillian Brown contributes an essay on "Hawthorne's American History." Karen Sánchez-Eppler takes another look at "Hawthorne and the Writing of Childhood." In essays devoted to the four major novels Brook Thomas analyzes "Love and Politics, Sympathy and Justice in *The Scarlet Letter*," Chris Castiglia explores "The Marvelous Queer Interiors of *The House of the Seven Gables*," Robert S. Levine looks at "Sympathy and Reform in *The Blithedale Romance*," and Emily Miller Budick offers "Perplexity, Sympathy, and the Question of the Human: a Reading of *The Marble Faun*." Finally, Gordon Hutner asks, "Whose Hawthorne?" in order to play off Lionel Trilling's essay, "Our Hawthorne," in the *Hawthorne Centenary Essays* (1964) and to survey the interaction among readers, their times, and their view of Hawthorne.

Also responsive to the Centenary Essays, which marked the one-hundredth anniversary of Hawthorne's death, Millicent Bell edited a collection of bicentennial essays, *Hawthorne and the Real* (2005), to honor the two hundredth anniversary of his birth. The collection includes work by ten scholars, including Bell ("Hawthorne and the Real"), Michael T. Gilmore ("Hawthorne and Politics [Again]: Words and Deeds in the 1850s"), Larry J. Reynolds ("'Strangely Ajar with the Human Race': Hawthorne, Slavery, and the Question of Moral Responsibility"), Lawrence Buell ("Hawthorne and the Problem of 'American' Fiction: the Example of *The Scarlet Letter*"), John Carlos Rowe ("Nathaniel Hawthorne and Transnationality"), Nina Baym ("Revisiting Hawthorne's Feminism"), David Leverenz ("Working Women and Creative Doubles: Getting to *The Marble Faun*"), Rita K. Gollin ("Estranged Allegiances in Hawthorne's Unfinished Romances"), Brenda Wineapple ("Nathaniel Hawthorne, Writer; or, the Fleeing of the Biographied"), and myself ("Hawthorne's Early Tales: Male Authorship, Domestic Violence, and Female Readers").

"The history of Hawthorne's genius is in some sense a summary of all New England's history," George Parsons Lathrop would write in his 1876 study of Hawthorne (8), but recent scholars have ranged much more widely in pursuing the author's relationship to history and culture. Studies of Hawthorne show no signs of diminishing, and it seems very likely that we shall see more scholarship that explores Hawthorne's connections to his nineteenth-century world. Whether or not Hawthorne's "genius" can be considered a summary of all *America's* history, scholarly studies that examine Hawthorne's relationship to American culture should flourish like rose bushes in the footsteps of Anne Hutchinson well into the twenty-first century.

Notes

1 Hawthorne's life

1. Brenda Wineapple, *Hawthorne: A Life* (New York: Knopf, 2003), 133.
2. Quoted in Sterling F. Delano, *Brook Farm: The Dark Side of Utopia* (Cambridge, MA: Belknap Press of Harvard University Press, 2004), 34.
3. See Philip McFarland, *Hawthorne in Concord* (New York: Grove Press, 2004) for a thorough account of Hawthorne's life in Concord in the 1840s, as well as in the last years of his life. Also see Carlos Baker, *Emerson among the Eccentrics: A Group Portrait* (New York: Viking, 1996).
4. Thomas R. Mitchell, *Hawthorne's Fuller Mystery* (Amherst: University of Massachusetts Press, 1998).
5. Hershel Parker, *Herman Melville: A Biography* (Baltimore: Johns Hopkins University Press, 1996), 1: 749.
6. Herman Melville, *Correspondence*, vol. 14 of *The Writings of Herman Melville*, ed. Harrison Hayford, Hershel Parker, and G. Thomas Tanselle (Evanston and Chicago: Northwestern University Press and the Newberry Library, 1993), 212.
7. Edwin H. Miller, *Melville* (New York: Persea, 1975), 249–50.
8. Parker, *Herman Melville: A Biography*, 1: 760.
9. Robert Milder, "'The Ugly Socrates': Melville, Hawthorne, and Homoeroticism," *ESQ* 46 (2000): 4.
10. Monica Mueller, *"This Infinite Fraternity of Feeling": Gender, Genre, and Homoerotic Crisis in Hawthorne's "The Blithedale Romance" and Melville's "Pierre"* (Madison: Fairleigh Dickinson University Press, 1996).
11. James Creech, *Closet Writing/Gay Reading: The Case of Melville's "Pierre"* (University of Chicago Press, 1993).
12. William Charvat, "Introduction," *The House of the Seven Gables*, vol. 2 of *The Centenary Edition of the Works of Nathaniel Hawthorne*, ed. William Charvat, Roy Harvey Pearce, and Claude M. Simpson (Columbus: Ohio State University Press, 1965), xx.
13. Jonathan Arac, "The Politics of *The Scarlet Letter*," *Ideology and Classic American Literature*, ed. Sacvan Bercovitch and Myra Jehlen (New York: Cambridge University Press, 1986), 247–66; Sacvan Bercovitch, *The Office of "The Scarlet Letter"*

(Baltimore: Johns Hopkins University Press, 1991). Arac compares Hawthorne's treatment of contemporary political issues, especially abolitionism, in *The Scarlet Letter* and *The Life of Franklin Pierce*. See chapter 2 of this book for more discussion of the two works.

14. The campaign biography, entitled *The Life of Franklin Pierce*, appears in *Miscellaneous Prose and Verse*, vol. 23 of *The Centenary Edition* (273–376).

15. *Nathaniel Hawthorne: The Contemporary Reviews*, ed. John L. Idol, Jr., and Buford Jones (New York: Cambridge University Press, 1994), 227, 231.

16. Vol. 17 of *The Centenary Edition*, *The Letters, 1853–1856*, includes a very useful chronology of Hawthorne's life from 1853 until his death in 1864 (pp. 87–97). I have relied on that chronology a great deal in summarizing the last decade of Hawthorne's life.

17. Hawthorne foresaw as much as $20,000 in a March 1855 letter to Ticknor (17: 318).

18. Hawthorne worked on that manuscript off and on for several years, including his first months in Italy, and then again after he returned to America. *The American Claimant Manuscripts*, vol. 12 of *The Centenary Edition* (1977), includes three manuscripts, "The Ancestral Footstep," "Etherege," and "Grimshawe" – all of them versions of the romance for which Hawthorne had the "germ" in 1855.

19. Hawthorne's preface appears in *Miscellaneous Prose and Verse* (23: 390–98).

20. Hawthorne described Lincoln as "being about the homeliest man I ever saw, yet by no means repulsive or disagreeable." Hawthorne also described his "lengthy awkwardness," the "uncouthness of his movement," and the "shabby slippers on his feet" (23: 412). See the "Historical and Textual Commentary" in *Miscellaneous Prose and Verse* for an account of the deletions (23: 689).

2 Hawthorne's contexts

1. Charles Ryskamp, "The New England Sources of *The Scarlet Letter*," *American Literature* 31 (1959): 257–72; Michael J. Colacurcio, "Footsteps of Ann Hutchinson: The Context of *The Scarlet Letter*," *ELH* 39 (1972): 459–94.

2. Perry Miller, *The New England Mind: The Seventeenth Century* (Cambridge, MA: Harvard University Press, 1939), 34.

3. David D. Hall, "Introduction," *The Antinomian Controversy, 1636–1638: A Documentary History*, ed. Hall, 2nd edn (Durham, NC: Duke University Press, 1990), 17.

4. David Levin, "Shadows of Doubt: Specter Evidence in Hawthorne's 'Young Goodman Brown,'" *American Literature* 34 (1962): 344–52.

5. For information about William Prynne see William Lamont, *Puritanism and Historical Controversy* (London: University College of London Press, 1996), 15–25, and Mukhtar Ali Isani, "Hawthorne and the Branding of William Prynne," *New England Quarterly* 45 (1972): 182–95.

6. Ralph Waldo Emerson, "The Divinity School Address," *Nature, Addresses, and Lectures*, ed. Robert E. Spiller and Alfred R. Ferguson (Cambridge, MA: Harvard University Press, 1979), 90.

7. Ralph Waldo Emerson, "Self-Reliance," *The Essays of Ralph Waldo Emerson*, ed. Alfred R. Ferguson and Jean Ferguson Carr (Cambridge, MA: Harvard University Press, 1987), 27.

8. Ralph Waldo Emerson, "The American Scholar," *Nature, Addresses, and Lectures*, ed. Spiller and Ferguson, 56.

9. Larry J. Reynolds, "Hawthorne's Labors in Concord," *The Cambridge Companion to Nathaniel Hawthorne*, ed. Richard H. Millington (Cambridge University Press, 2004), 16.

10. See, for example, Alison Easton, "Hawthorne and the Question of Women," *The Cambridge Companion to Nathaniel Hawthorne*, ed. Millington, 79–98, for a very informative account of Hawthorne's engagement with the "Woman Question."

11. Nina Baym has made the case for Hawthorne as a feminist writer in several essays and books, most recently in "Revisiting Hawthorne's Feminism," *Nathaniel Hawthorne Review* 30 (2004), 32–55.

12. Leslie Fiedler, *Love and Death in the American Novel* (New York: Dell, 1966), most famously catalogues and analyzes the role of Fair Maidens and Dark Ladies in the works of nineteenth-century male authors, including Hawthorne. See also Judith Fryer, *The Faces of Eve: Women in the Nineteenth-Century American Novel* (New York: Oxford University Press, 1976), and Joyce W. Warren, *The American Narcissus: Individualism and Women in Nineteenth-Century American Fiction* (New Brunswick: Rutgers University Press, 1984).

13. Toni Morrison, *Playing in the Dark: Whiteness and the Literary Imagination* (Cambridge, MA: Harvard University Press, 1992), 46–47.

14. Arac, "The Politics of *The Scarlet Letter*," 251.

15. Bercovitch, *The Office of "The Scarlet Letter*," 89, 109, 110.

16. Jean Fagan Yellin, "Hawthorne and the American National Sin," *The Green American Tradition: Essays and Poems for Sherman Paul*, ed. H. Daniel Peck (Baton Rouge: Louisiana State University Press, 1989), 75–97, and *Women and Sisters: The Antislavery Feminists in American Culture* (New Haven: Yale University Press, 1989).

17. Yellin, *Women and Sisters*, 138. Yellin goes on, however, to argue that Hester's refusal to become a prophetess at the end of the novel reflects Hawthorne's repudiation of the "antislavery feminists who were defying social taboos in an effort to move other women to action" (149).

18. David Anthony, "Class, Culture, and the Trouble with White Skin in Hawthorne's *The House of the Seven Gables*," *The House of the Seven Gables*, ed. Robert S. Levine (New York: W. W. Norton, 2006), 439–40.

19. Larry J. Reynolds, "'Strangely Ajar with the Human Race': Hawthorne, Slavery, and the Question of Moral Responsibility," *Hawthorne and the Real: Bicentennial Essays*, ed. Millicent Bell (Columbus: Ohio State University Press, 2005), 48.

20. Nancy Bentley, *The Ethnography of Manners: Hawthorne, James, Wharton* (New York: Cambridge University Press, 1995), 24–25.

21. Wineapple, *Hawthorne: A Life*, cites Garrison's objections to Hawthorne's comment (351) but credits Hawthorne with a "fine-tuned perception of America's heritage." "These unequal terms are his point," she writes. "And what he means by unequal terms lies at the heart of a national hypocrisy that, in one incarnation or another, has always been Hawthorne's subject, whether he writes about Puritans, Tories, rebels, or transcendentalists" (350).

22. Kimmel, *Manhood in America: A Cultural History* (New York: Free Press, 1996), 9.

23. T. Walter Herbert, "Hawthorne and American Masculinity," *The Cambridge Companion to Nathaniel Hawthorne*, ed. Millington, 60, 76.

24. See Michael Winship, "Hawthorne and the 'Scribbling Women': Publishing *The Scarlet Letter* in the Nineteenth-Century United States," *Studies in American Fiction* 29 (2001): 3–11.

25. Margaret Fuller, *The Letters of Margaret Fuller*, ed. Robert N. Hudspeth, 4 vols. (Ithaca: Cornell University Press, 1983–87), 1: 198; Longfellow, Review of *Twice-Told Tales* (1842), in *The Recognition of Nathaniel Hawthorne*, ed. B. Bernard Cohen (Ann Arbor: University of Michigan Press, 1969), 10.

26. T. Walter Herbert, *Dearest Beloved: The Hawthornes and the Making of the Middle-Class Family* (Berkeley: University of California Press, 1993), 71.

3 Hawthorne's short fiction

1. With its college setting, *Fanshawe* derives from Hawthorne's college experience at Bowdoin and interests Hawthorne scholars today mainly because of the way its male and female characters anticipate those in his short fiction and major novels.

2. J. Donald Crowley, "Historical Commentary," *Twice-Told Tales*, vol. 9 of *The Centenary Edition*, 503, 504.

3. Quoted in Peter Balakian, "Two Lost Letters: Hawthorne at College; Longfellow and Hawthorne: the Beginning of a Friendship," *New England Quarterly* 56 (1983): 431.

4. Henry Wadsworth Longfellow, Review of *Twice-Told Tales*, *North American Review* 45 (July 1837): 60.

5. Barbara Welter, *Dimity Convictions: The American Woman in the Nineteenth Century* (Athens: Ohio University Press, 1976), 21.

6. Leland Person, "Hawthorne's Early Tales: Male Authorship, Domestic Violence, and Female Readers," *Hawthorne and the Real: Bicentennial Essays*, ed. Bell, 125–43. I have adapted my discussion of Hawthorne's early tales from this essay.

7. Christopher Packard, "Who's Laughing Now? Sentimental Readers and Authorial Revenge in 'Alice Doane's Appeal,'" *Arizona Quarterly* 52 (1996): 5.

8. Mary Ventura, "'Alice Doane's Appeal': the Seducer Revealed," *ATQ* 10 (1996): 29.

9. Michael J. Colacurcio, *The Province of Piety: Moral History in Hawthorne's Early Tales* (Cambridge, MA: Harvard University Press, 1984), 109.

10. Frederick Crews, *The Sins of the Fathers: Hawthorne's Psychological Themes* (New York: Oxford University Press, 1966), 88.

11. See especially David Levin, "Shadows of Doubt: Specter Evidence in Hawthorne's 'Young Goodman Brown,'" *American Literature* 34 (1962): 344–52, and Colacurcio, *Province*, 283–313.

12. *The American Notebooks*, ed. Claude M. Simpson, vol. 8 of *The Centenary Edition*, 22. Subsequent references by volume and page.

13. Edgar Allan Poe, Review of *Twice-Told Tales*, in *Nathaniel Hawthorne's Tales*, ed. James McIntosh (New York: W. W. Norton, 1987), 331.

14. J. Hillis Miller, *Hawthorne and History: Defacing It* (Cambridge, MA: Basil Blackwell, 1991), 105.

15. John F. Birk, "Hawthorne's Mister Hooper: the Veil of Ham?" *Prospects* 21 (1996): 1–11.

16. Sharon Cameron, *The Corporeal Self: Allegories of the Body in Melville and Hawthorne* (Baltimore: Johns Hopkins University Press, 1981), 130.

17. *The Snow-Image and Uncollected Tales*, vol. 11 of *The Centenary Edition*, 209.

18. Frederick Crews, *The Sins of the Fathers: Hawthorne's Psychological Themes* (New York: Oxford University Press, 1966), 73, 78.

19. Herbert, "Hawthorne and American Masculinity," *The Cambridge Companion to Nathaniel Hawthorne*, ed. Millington, 66.

20. Emerson, "Self-Reliance," *The Essays of Ralph Waldo Emerson*, ed. Ferguson and Carr, 27.

21. David Leverenz, *Manhood and the American Renaissance* (Ithaca: Cornell University Press, 1989), 231.

22. Sylvester Graham, *A Lecture to Young Men* (Providence: Weeden and Cory, 1834; reprinted Arno Press, 1974), 25.

23. Herman Melville, "Hawthorne and His Mosses," *The Piazza Tales and Other Prose Pieces, 1839–1860*, vol. 9 of *The Writings of Herman Melville*, ed. Harrison Hayford, Alma A. MacDougall, and G. Thomas Tanselle (Evanston and Chicago: Northwestern University Press and the Newberry Library, 1987), 243.

24. Margaret Fuller, *Woman in the Nineteenth Century*, ed. Larry J. Reynolds (New York: W. W. Norton, 1998), 102.

25. Judith Fetterley, *The Resisting Reader: A Feminist Approach to American Fiction* (Bloomington: Indiana University Press, 1978), 22–23, 24.

26. Michael Davitt Bell, *The Development of American Romance: The Sacrifice of Relation* (University of Chicago Press, 1980), 138.

27. I have argued this idea at greater length in "Hawthorne's Bliss of Paternity: Sophia's Absence from 'The Old Manse,'" *Studies in the Novel* 23 (Spring 1991): 46–59. Brenda Wineapple also sees Owen Warland's manufacture of the butterfly as a pregnancy fantasy: "Owen becomes ill, gains weight, grows plump – after which episode he does eventually succeed in crafting (giving birth) to a beautiful little thing" (*Hawthorne: A Life*, 176).

28. Mitchell, *Hawthorne's Fuller Mystery*, 107.

29. Carol Bensick, *La Nouvelle Beatrice: Renaissance and Romance in "Rappaccini's Daughter"* (New Brunswick: Rutgers University Press, 1985); Dawn Keetley, "Beautiful Poisoners: 'Rappaccini's Daughter,' Hannah Kinney's 1840 Murder Trial, and the Problems of Criminal Responsibility," *ESQ* 44 (1998): 125–59.

30. Richard Brenzo, "Beatrice Rappaccini: a Victim of Male Love and Horror," *American Literature* 48 (1976): 157.

31. Anna Brickhouse, "'I Do Abhor an Indian Story': Hawthorne and the Allegorization of Racial 'Commixture,'" *ESQ* 42 (1996): 240.

4 Hawthorne's novels

1. Arthur Cleveland Coxe, from *The Church Review*, *"The Scarlet Letter" and Other Writings*, ed. Leland S. Person (New York: W. W. Norton, 2005), 258–59.

2. See Louise K. Barnett, "Speech and Society in *The Scarlet Letter*," *ESQ: A Journal of the American Renaissance* 29 (1983): 16–24.

3. Michael Small, "Hawthorne's *The Scarlet Letter*: Arthur Dimmesdale's Manipulation of Language," *American Imago* 37 (1980), 115.

4. See my essay, "Hester's Revenge: the Power of Silence in *The Scarlet Letter*," *Nineteenth-Century Literature* 43 (1989): 465–83.

5. See my essay, "*The Scarlet Letter* and the Myth of the Divine Child," *American Transcendental Quarterly* 44 (1979): 295–309.

6. See my essay, "Inscribing Paternity: Nathaniel Hawthorne as a Nineteenth-Century Father," *Studies in the American Renaissance*, ed. Joel Myerson (Charlottesville: University Press of Virginia, 1991), 217–36.

7. Rose Hawthorne Lathrop, *Memories of Hawthorne* (Boston: Houghton, Mifflin, 1897), 88.

8. Henry Clarke Wright, *Marriage and Parentage: or, the Reproductive Element in Man, as a Means to His Elevation and Happiness*, 2nd edn (Boston: Bela Marsh, 1855; rpt. New York: Arno Press, 1974), 4, 5.

9. Nina Baym has recently argued that Hepzibah is Hawthorne's heroine, in part because, in standing up to Jaffrey, she indirectly causes his death. See "The Heroine of *The House of the Seven Gables*: or, Who Killed Jaffrey Pyncheon?" *New England Quarterly* 77 (2004): 607–18.

10. Anthony, "Class, Culture, and the Trouble with White Skin in Hawthorne's *The House of the Seven Gables*," *The House of the Seven Gables*, ed. Levine, 447.

11. Amy Schrager Lang, *The Syntax of Class: Writing Inequality in Nineteenth-Century America* (Princeton University Press, 2003), 37–38.

12. Samuel Chase Coale, *Mesmerism and Hawthorne: Mediums of American Romance* (Tuscaloosa: University of Alabama Press, 1998), 3.

13. Chris Castiglia, "The Marvelous Queer Interiors of *The House of the Seven Gables*," *The Cambridge Companion to Nathaniel Hawthorne*, ed. Millington, 187.

14. Susan Williams, "'The Aspiring Purpose of an Ambitious Demagogue': Portraiture and *The House of the Seven Gables*," *Nineteenth-Century Literature* 49 (1994): 227.

15. Alan Trachtenberg, "Seeing and Believing: Hawthorne's Reflections on the Daguerreotype in *The House of the Seven Gables*," *The House of the Seven Gables*, ed. Levine, 419.

16. Cathy Davidson, "Photographs of the Dead: Sherman, Daguerre, Hawthorne," *South Atlantic Quarterly* 89 (1990): 690.

17. Gillian Brown, *Domestic Individualism: Imagining Self in Nineteenth-Century America* (Berkeley: University of California Press, 1990), 69.

18. *The Blithedale Romance and Fanshawe*, vol. 3 of *The Centenary Edition* (1).

19. Robert Martin, "Hester Prynne, *C'est Moi*: Nathaniel Hawthorne and the Anxieties of Gender," *Engendering Men: The Question of Male Feminist Criticism*, ed. Joseph A. Boone and Michael Cadden (New York: Routledge, 1990), 132.

20. Melville, "Hawthorne and His Mosses," 241, 250.

21. Herman Melville, *Moby-Dick; or, The Whale*, vol. 6 in *The Writings of Herman Melville*, ed. Hayford, Parker, and Tanselle, 163.

22. Edwin Miller, *Salem Is My Dwelling Place: A Life of Nathaniel Hawthorne* (Iowa City: University of Iowa Press, 1991), 357.

23. Mueller, *This Infinite Fraternity of Feeling*, 22.

24. Nina Baym, *The Shape of Hawthorne's Career* (Ithaca: Cornell University Press, 1976), 190.

25. Mary Suzanne Schriber, "Justice to Zenobia," *New England Quarterly* 55 (1982): 68.

26. Louise DeSalvo, *Nathaniel Hawthorne* (Atlantic Highlands: Humanities Press International, 1987), 111. For the "murder" case against Coverdale, see John Harmon McElroy and Edward L. McDonald, "The Coverdale Romance," *Studies in the Novel* 14 (1982): 1–16, and Beverly Hume, "Restructuring the Case against Hawthorne's Coverdale," *Nineteenth-Century Fiction* 40 (1986): 387–99.

27. Henry James, *Hawthorne* (London: Macmillan, 1879), 165.

28. Baym, *Shape*, 236.

29. For a more extended discussion of Hawthorne's conflicted response to the sculpture he encountered in Italy, see my essay, "Falling into Heterosexuality: Sculpting Male Bodies in *The Marble Faun* and *Roderick Hudson*," *Roman Holidays: American Writers and Artists in Nineteenth-Century Italy*, ed. Robert K. Martin and Leland S. Person (Iowa City: University of Iowa Press, 2002), 107–39.

30. Joy S. Kasson, *Marble Queens and Captives: Women in Nineteenth-Century American Sculpture* (New Haven: Yale University Press, 1990).

31. Abigail Solomon-Godeau, *Male Trouble: A Crisis in Representation* (New York: Thames and Hudson, 1997), 25–26.

32. Bentley, *The Ethnography of Manners: Hawthorne, James, Wharton*; Kristie Hamilton, "Fauns and Mohicans: Narratives of Extinction and Hawthorne's Aesthetic of Modernity," *Roman Holidays: American Writers and Artists in Nineteenth-Century Italy*, ed. Martin and Person, 41–59.

Guide to further reading

Barlowe, Jamie. *The Scarlet Mob of Scribblers: Rereading Hester Prynne.*
Carbondale: Southern Illinois University Press, 2000. Provocative
feminist study that includes a very interesting analysis of *The Scarlet
Letter* and the 1995 movie version of the novel.

Baym, Nina. *"The Scarlet Letter": A Reading.* Boston: Twayne, 1986. Excellent
introductory book on *The Scarlet Letter* by one of Hawthorne's best
critics.

The Shape of Hawthorne's Career. Ithaca: Cornell University Press, 1976. A
groundbreaking study of Hawthorne when first published. Especially
good insights into the role Hawthorne's women characters play in his
major fiction.

Bell, Millicent, ed. *New Essays on Hawthorne's Major Tales.* New York: Cambridge
University Press, 1993. Includes five essays by well-known scholars, with
attention to "Rappaccini's Daughter," "The Minister's Black Veil,"
"Ethan Brand," "My Kinsman, Major Molineux," "Roger Malvin's
Burial," "The Celestial Railroad," and "Young Goodman Brown."

Hawthorne and the Real: Bicentennial Essays. Columbus: Ohio State
University Press, 2005. Written in honor of Hawthorne's two-hundredth
birthday, a dozen essays on various topics by prominent Hawthorne
scholars.

Bercovitch, Sacvan. *The Office of "The Scarlet Letter".* Baltimore: Johns Hopkins
University Press, 1991. Very influential study, exemplifying New
Historicist cultural approach. Examines the novel in light of
nineteenth-century politics and finds it to be in league with desires to
"embrace gradualism and consensus" on issues such as slavery.

Berlant, Lauren. *The Anatomy of National Fantasy: Hawthorne, Utopia, and
Everyday Life.* University of Chicago Press, 1991. Ranges between
seventeenth- and nineteenth-century moments to explore Hawthorne's
politics, particularly his representation of citizenship.

Brodhead, Richard. *The School of Hawthorne.* New York: Oxford University Press,
1986. Emphasis on Herman Melville, William Dean Howells, Henry
James, and William Faulkner and their fictional responses to
Hawthorne's example.

Budick, Emily Miller. *Engendering Romance: Women Writers and the Hawthorne
Tradition, 1850–1990.* New Haven: Yale University Press, 1994. Places

Hawthorne at the head of a female tradition of romance writing that includes Carson McCullers, Flannery O'Connor, Toni Morrison, and Grace Paley (as well as Henry James and William Faulkner).

Buitenhuis, Peter. *"The House of the Seven Gables": Severing Family and Colonial Ties*. Boston: Twayne, 1991. Good introductory study of Hawthorne's second novel.

Cain, William E., ed. *The Blithedale Romance*. A Bedford Cultural Edition. Boston: Bedford Books, 1996. Includes very useful background information on utopianism, as well as nineteenth-century political and economic theories.

Carton, Evan. *"The Marble Faun": Hawthorne's Transformations*. New York: Twayne, 1992. Excellent introductory study of Hawthorne's last novel, emphasizing its engagement with nineteenth-century American issues.

Coale, Samuel Chase. *In Hawthorne's Shadow: American Romance from Melville to Mailer*. Lexington: University Press of Kentucky, 1985. Wide-ranging study of Hawthorne's influence on such twentieth-century writers as William Faulkner, William Styron, Flannery O'Connor, John Cheever, John Updike, Norman Mailer, and others.

Mesmerism and Hawthorne: Mediums of American Romance. Tuscaloosa: University of Alabama Press, 1998. Useful account of Hawthorne's interest in and use of mesmerism in many of his works.

Colacurcio, Michael J. *The Province of Piety: Moral History in Hawthorne's Early Tales*. Cambridge, MA: Harvard University Press, 1984. Meticulously studies Hawthorne's knowledge of historical sources in stories such as "Young Goodman Brown," "The Minister's Black Veil," "My Kinsman, Major Molineux," "Wakefield," "Roger Malvin's Burial," "The Gentle Boy," and others.

Colacurcio, Michael J., ed. *New Essays on "The Scarlet Letter"*. New York: Cambridge University Press, 1985. Includes four essays on the novel, including one by Colacurcio.

Crews, Frederick. *The Sins of the Fathers: Hawthorne's Psychological Themes*. New York: Oxford University Press, 1966. A provocative Freudian study of Hawthorne's writing; excellent psychoanalytic analyses of tales and novels.

Dauber, Kenneth. *Rediscovering Hawthorne*. Princeton University Press, 1977. Emphasizes Hawthorne's poetics, discounting his "visionary" tendencies, in favor of a structuralist approach that discovers stories layered one upon the other.

Davis, Clark. *Hawthorne's Shyness: Ethics, Politics, and the Question of Engagement*. Baltimore: Johns Hopkins University Press, 2005. In contrast to recent studies critical of Hawthorne's politics, emphasizes Hawthorne's engagement – and complex depiction of engagement – with ethical questions.

DeSalvo, Louise. *Nathaniel Hawthorne*. Atlantic Highlands: Humanities Press, 1987. An important feminist study critical of Hawthorne's attitudes toward women.

Easton, Alison. *The Making of the Hawthorne Subject*. Columbia: University of
Missouri Press, 1996. Especially valuable study of Hawthorne's early
development as a writer and his efforts to devise a viable authorial
"self."

Erlich, Gloria C. *Family Themes and Hawthorne's Fiction: The Tenacious Web*.
New Brunswick: Rutgers University Press, 1984. Part biography, part
criticism. Emphasizes Hawthorne's early childhood experiences and
three themes: maternal deprivation, paternal loss, and domination by
stepfather figures.

Gale, Robert L. *A Nathaniel Hawthorne Encyclopedia*. Boston: G. K. Hall, 1991.
Very important reference source. Includes detailed entries on just about
everything a reader might think of asking about.

Herbert, T. Walter. *Dearest Beloved: The Hawthornes and the Making of the
Middle-Class Family*. Berkeley: University of California Press, 1993.
Provocative family biography that portrays Hawthorne and his wife as
victims of nineteenth-century separate spheres ideologies that in turn
victimize their children. Keys each of four sections to one of the major
romances.

Hutner, Gordon. *Secrets and Sympathy: Forms of Disclosure in Hawthorne's Novels*.
Athens: University of Georgia Press, 1988. Sympathy enables characters
to cross the boundary between themselves and ourselves and so achieve
understanding and knowledge.

Idol, John L., Jr., and Melinda Ponder, eds. *Hawthorne and Women: Engendering
and Expanding the Hawthorne Tradition*. Amherst: University of
Massachusetts Press, 1999. Important collection of essays on
Hawthorne's relationship to certain women, as well as on his influence
on many women writers.

Idol, John L., Jr., and Buford Jones, eds. *Nathaniel Hawthorne: The Contemporary
Reviews*. New York: Cambridge University Press, 1994. Very good,
although not complete, collection of early reviews of Hawthorne's
publications.

Johnson, Claudia Durst, ed. *Understanding "The Scarlet Letter": A Student
Casebook to Issues, Sources, and Historical Documents*. Westport:
Greenwood, 1995. Includes excerpts from seventeenth-century,
nineteenth-century, and even twentieth-century documents to aid
readers in developing various historical contexts for understanding the
novel.

Kesterson, David B., ed. *Critical Essays on Hawthorne's "The Scarlet Letter"*.
Boston: G. K. Hall, 1988. Good collection of previously published essays.

Laffrado, Laura. *Hawthorne's Literature for Children*. Athens: University of
Georgia Press, 1992. The only book-length study of Hawthorne's several
collections of tales for children.

Leverenz, David. *Manhood and the American Renaissance*. Ithaca: Cornell
University Press, 1989. Very important study of nineteenth-century
American literature and its engagement with questions about manhood.
Includes two insightful chapters on Hawthorne.

Levine, Robert S., ed. *The House of the Seven Gables*. New York: W. W. Norton, 2006. Norton Critical Edition includes many important essays and background information on the novel.

Luedtke, Luther S. *Nathaniel Hawthorne and the Romance of the Orient.* Bloomington: Indiana University Press, 1989. Fascinating study emphasizing Hawthorne's knowledge of Oriental history and culture – his knowledge of *The Arabian Nights*, for example.

McWilliams, John P., Jr. *Hawthorne, Melville, and the American Character: A Looking-Glass Business*. Cambridge University Press, 1984. Demonstrates connections in Hawthorne's fiction among seventeenth-century, eighteenth-century, and nineteenth-century moments in American history.

Martin, Terence. *Nathaniel Hawthorne*. Revised Edition. Boston: Twayne, 1983. Excellent introduction to Hawthorne's major works.

Mellow, James R. *Nathaniel Hawthorne in His Times*. Boston: Houghton Mifflin, 1980. The most comprehensive Hawthorne biography, with detailed treatment of many important events in Hawthorne's life.

Miller, Edwin Haviland. *Salem Is My Dwelling Place: A Life of Nathaniel Hawthorne*. Iowa City: University of Iowa Press, 1991. Biographical study that sees Hawthorne as a "gentle boy" anxious about his sexuality and his manliness. Provocative speculations on the homoerotic dimensions of Hawthorne's friendship with Melville.

Miller, J. Hillis. *Hawthorne and History: Defacing It*. Cambridge, MA: Basil Blackwell, 1991. Focuses on "The Minister's Black Veil" and the theory of history and historical knowledge that may be inferred from it. Concludes that all signs are potentially unreadable, or that the reading of them is potentially unverifiable.

Millington, Richard H. *Practicing Romance: Narrative Form and Cultural Engagement in Hawthorne's Fiction*. Princeton University Press, 1992. Synthesizes Freudian psychoanalysis, New Historicism, reader-response theory, and other critical methodologies to examine the interplay of individual and society in Hawthorne's fiction.

Millington, Richard H., ed. *The Cambridge Companion to Nathaniel Hawthorne*. Cambridge University Press, 2004. Excellent collection of a dozen topical essays by prominent scholars, each of them coming at Hawthorne from a different cultural angle.

Mitchell, Thomas R. *Hawthorne's Fuller Mystery*. Amherst: University of Massachusetts Press, 1998. Very provocative book that argues for Margaret Fuller's influence on Hawthorne and his writing. Sees Fuller in "Rappaccini's Daughter" and in the four novels.

Moore, Margaret B. *The Salem World of Nathaniel Hawthorne*. Columbia: University of Missouri Press, 1998. Biographical study of Hawthorne's Salem background.

Newman, Lea Bertani Vozar. *A Reader's Guide to the Short Stories of Nathaniel Hawthorne*. Boston: G. K. Hall, 1979. A still useful survey of criticism on every one of Hawthorne's short works.

Person, Leland S. *Aesthetic Headaches: Women and a Masculine Poetics in Poe, Melville, and Hawthorne*. Athens: University of Georgia Press, 1988. Includes three chapters on Hawthorne's major women characters.

Person, Leland S., ed. *"The Scarlet Letter" and Other Writings*. New York: W. W. Norton, 2005. Norton Critical Edition includes many important essays on the novel and on selected shorter works.

Pfister, Joel. *The Production of Personal Life: Class, Gender, and the Psychological in Hawthorne's Fiction*. Stanford University Press, 1991. Historicizes Hawthornian psychology by focusing on the intersection of gender and class (especially new middle-class domestic values) in Hawthorne's fiction.

Reynolds, Larry J., ed. *A Historical Guide to Nathaniel Hawthorne*. New York: Oxford University Press, 2001. Four essays situate Hawthorne's writing in relation to mesmerism, the visual arts, changing ideas about child-rearing, and the slavery question.

Rosenthal, Bernard, ed. *Critical Essays on Hawthorne's "The House of the Seven Gables"*. New York: G. K. Hall, 1995. Excellent collection of previously published essays.

Scharnhorst, Gary, ed. *The Critical Response to Nathaniel Hawthorne's "The Scarlet Letter"*. Westport: Greenwood, 1992. Very useful collection of reviews, especially nineteenth-century reviews of Hawthorne's most famous novel.

Schiff, James. *Updike's Version: Rewriting "The Scarlet Letter"*. Columbia: University of Missouri Press, 1992. Excellent study of John Updike's three "scarlet letter" novels, *A Month of Sundays*, *Roger's Version*, and *S*.

Thompson, G. R. *The Art of Authorial Presence: Hawthorne's Provincial Tales*. Durham, NC: Duke University Press, 1993. Considers Hawthorne a crafty manipulator of narrative voice in eight early tales, including "Alice Doane's Appeal," "Roger Malvin's Burial," "The Gentle Boy," and "My Kinsman, Major Molineux."

Turner, Arlin. *Nathaniel Hawthorne: A Biography*. New York: Oxford University Press, 1980. Excellent biography.

von Frank, Albert J., ed. *Critical Essays on Hawthorne's Short Stories*. Boston: G. K. Hall, 1991. Good collection of previously published essays.

Wilson, James C. *The Hawthorne and Melville Friendship: An Annotated Bibliography, Biographical and Critical Essays, and Correspondence Between the Two*. Jefferson: McFarland, 1991. Good collection of documents and early critical studies of the Hawthorne–Melville relationship.

Wineapple, Brenda. *Hawthorne: A Life*. New York: Alfred A. Knopf, 2003. Excellent recent biography, especially good on Hawthorne's attitudes toward race, slavery, and abolition.

Index